Fixing America's Shattered Politics

To Ron,
Thank you for your Service!

Fixing America's Shattered Politics

PRACTICAL STEPS CONCERNED CITIZENS CAN TAKE TO REGAIN OUR LOST GOVERNMENT

. . .

Alan Duff

ISBN: 1532905467
ISBN 13: 9781532905469
Library of Congress Control Number: 2016906868
CreateSpace Independent Publishing Platform
North Charleston, South Carolina

What others are saying about *Fixing America's Shattered Politics*

"To a man who is willing to go against the grain and give us information that most politicians want to hide from us shows great boldness, resiliency, courage and love for his country. Thank you for being the man of God that you are and holding fast to the truth!"

Sheila Raye Charles, Singer, Author and Daughter of Ray Charles

"What has become painfully apparent to even the most casual observer, our government at all levels has lost their way and become devoid of many of the values of our founding fathers. As a military veteran and one who has won elected office, US Army Reserve Major (Ret) Alan Duff not only does a superb job of outlining how many of our politicians lack values such as integrity, honesty and selfless service but identifies his solutions to fix our utterly shattered politics and regain the trust of all Americans. BRAVO ZULU, Maj (Ret) Duff, BRAVO ZULU!"

Dennis Davis, former USAFR Captain and author of Not your Average Joe: Profiles of Military Core Values and Why They Matter in The Private Sector

"Fixing America's Shattered Politics is a book that could be written in every state, in almost every jurisdiction. In a time where left v right dominates the headlines, this book offers many practical non-partisan solutions."

Blake Huffman, Ramsey County Commissioner and Minnesota Veterans Journey

"Alan's combined background in military service and local politics allows him to bring great insights into the problems and necessary solutions for bringing America back to greatness. He is a true Patriot and honorable public servant for America!"

Jerry Kyser, US Army Vietnam Veteran and Ellis Island Award Recipient

"Fixing America's Shattered Politics is a book that should be mandatory reading in every high school Political Science & ROTC classrooms and Military Academies. If a volunteer is going to raise their hands to defend the U.S. Constitution and try to make a difference in America, then they need to go into it with both eyes open! Great Job MAJ Duff!"

Larry Josephs, United States Army First Sergeant - 1966-1995 (Ret.) Former Alderman, West St. Paul, MN

"American military veterans have earned our trust through dedicated service to the greater good and many politicians have not. With a strong background in public service through 23 years of military service, Alan provides exceptional ideas that empower concerned citizens to take effective steps in fixing our shattered politics."

Joe Johnson, Founder of Trust Vets

"Alan's brutal honesty about the concerns of politics today is something America needs to hear, and his ideas for fixing our shattered politics provide excellent tools for concerned citizens overseeing all political offices throughout the US."

Craig Johnson, Concerned Citizen

"Mr. Duff dealt with some unbelievable corruption in Isanti County, but these political problems are all around us in America today. His common-sense ideas for improving the lost trust between frustrated citizens and self-serving elected officials are needed ASAP at nearly every political level."

Jim Kennedy, former Isanti City Councilmember

"Al was subjected to some eye opening corruption at a County level, but this happens everywhere throughout the US. When a country is so focused on a bipartisan Presidential election, eyes become less focused on local, county and state politics; all of which have a major impact on citizens' everyday lives. Al does a fantastic job of providing a non-partisan, militarily focused plan to improve the service of these vital government levels."

Jeff Duncan, Concerned Citizen

"Al Duff leads by example! I have had the opportunity to work with Al on many occasions and his dedication to our veterans, community and our country is unmatched. He does a great job of identifying the negative impacts from corruption and presents many exceptional ideas on how concerned citizens can curtail the destruction caused by self-serving politicians."

Jeff Kolb, former Isanti City Councilmember

"At a time when our politicians seem to be failing at every level to provide leadership based on rationality and common sense, Alan Duff offers a brilliant set of ideas that all of America should take time to ponder. Kudos Alan for a phenomenal book, for your lifetime of service, and for sharing the truth when so many others are afraid to do so.

David Meece, Christian Music Hall of Famer

Dedication

. . .

This book is written in honor of the US military service members who made the ultimate sacrifice in defense of our nation.

I would also like to dedicate this book to two very special military veterans who were very instrumental in my life: Merle Duff, father and Army veteran, who taught me what it means to be a patriot (1943–2011), and Bob Ouimette, adopted grandfather and Navy veteran, who taught me what it means to be a humble servant (1923–2015).

Tomb of the Unknown Soldier,
Arlington, Virginia

Special Thanks

. . .

I WANT TO PERSONALLY THANK several individuals who provided great assistance in compiling this manuscript, including Louise Duff, loving wife, best friend, and my princess; Sandy Duff, loving mother; Brian Fanning, Army veteran and great friend; Dennis Davis, Air Force veteran and author; Todd Shaffer, Navy veteran and great friend; Craig Johnson, concerned citizen and great friend; and Lee Swanson, uncle and great patriot.

This book was written with love and a strong passion for improving America's future for my children, Hannah, Megan, Blake, Nathan, Cody and my grandchildren, Mercedes and Jaydon.

Contents

PART 1

An Inside Look at America's Shattered Politics

Introduction: The Biggest Threat
Facing America Today

• • •

In 1982, I TOOK AN oath for the US military to defend our nation against all enemies, both foreign and domestic. In the 1980s, our enemy was the potential spread of communism. In the 1990s, we fought over oil. Early in the first decade of the twenty-first century, symbolic US landmarks were attacked on 9-11, and we began a new war against terrorism. In the decade following 2010, I believe that the greatest enemy facing America is self-serving politicians who are damaging the sustainability of a once-great nation. And the data seems to prove that I am not alone in this thought. Poll after poll shows an alarming distrust and lack of respect for politicians. In fact, a Gallup poll taken from December 5–8, 2013, shows that *"72% of Americans think that big government is the greatest threat to the future of the US."*[1] So what is behind this problem, and, more importantly, how do we get out of this mess that is threatening the future of our nation?

At heart, I am a patriot who has an unending love for the great nation of America. I proudly served for twenty-three years in the US military to help protect our great nation and the things that it stood for, especially freedom and liberty to pursue a meaningful life. Fundamentally, I believe that America's foundation was built with a focus on self-reliance, which fosters a fair and great opportunity for all of our citizens to prosper.

America has a lengthy history of rags-to-riches stories that has withstood the test of time for well over two centuries.

I had a desire to continue my public service in local politics following my military service. After two years in city government, I was encouraged to run for a higher office as a county commissioner. After reviewing whether or not to pursue this elected office with several of my advisors, I was warned that our county was very corrupt and had many problems. Being an optimistic person, I thought it could not be that bad, especially since most of the local levels of government I had worked with had problems, but, overall, they functioned relatively well. I ran and won this county office position, and I was in for a rude awakening. The advice I was given covered only a small portion of the unbelievable dysfunctional and self-serving aspects of government that so many of us fear when it comes to our political leaders.

It was during these four years of working with the most dysfunctional board of elected officials I had ever worked with that I first realized that the nation I so dearly loved was under serious attack, and it was not from an outside enemy but rather from within. Politicians were taking over more and more of our lives and damaging the foundation of a great nation. After watching four years of political abuses that would be grounds for termination or lawsuits in the private sector or nonprofit world, I recognized that this form of "public service" was vastly different than military service. The former promoted self-serving interests while the later sacrificially guarded our nation.

Over the past four years, as I spoke about the corruption and dysfunction of our county government with other political experts across the nation, I sadly found out that our dysfunction was fairly common within other political jurisdictions throughout the United States. Whether at the county, state, federal, or another level of government, political abuse and dysfunction are hurting the once-stable foundation of our nation, changing it from one focused on freedom and limited government to one with extensive political abuse and fewer freedoms for our citizens.

With federal, state, and local taxes, the average American is paying well over a third of their income to taxes, and this is simply unsustainable. The United States was brilliantly designed to be governed by those officials closest to and elected by the people, yet today 55 percent of our taxes go to our federal government, while 45 percent go to our state and local governments.

Many are close to giving up on our future, but we have 240 years as a great nation, and the fight for the next years, decades, and, God willing, centuries must take place soon, or we will break down from within. I continue to be an eternal optimist that America will overcome its current problem of shattered politics that is destroying us and will do what America does best: overcome adversity and become an even stronger nation.

The problems identified in this book are written from a more detailed viewpoint of local government since that is where I served for six years following my military retirement. I believe that this is important because much has been written about the political system at the federal level but less has been said about the dysfunctions at other levels.

Besides, the examples of public abuse by the political elite are similar at virtually every level of US politics today, and local government is often the breeding ground for many future politicians. In fact, it was very disheartening for me to hear that there are many political organizations that are even more dysfunctional than what I experienced that highlights the depth and magnitude of the systemic problems within our overall political system. Our shattered politics has us, the citizens, in the grasp of its ever-increasing control at many levels, and it is time for America to wake up before our freedoms are completely eradicated.

My recommendations for fixing America's shattered politics are not based on political correctness or other related factors but rather are built from a military perspective. I contrast the extremely different values of self-serving politicians to sacrificial and selfless military service members. Thankfully, the defense of our nation is in good hands with our brave men and women in uniform, but the freedoms they fight for are rapidly being taken away by the political elite.

I wrote this book with the following goals in mind:

* To clarify the magnitude of the internal collapse within America's shattered politics
* To provide motivation for citizens by showing how we can slow this rapid downward spiral of our shattered politics, which is harming the foundation of America
* To help restore the seemingly lost hope that America can be a better place for future generations

It is high time we reverse this downward spiral before it's too late.

CHAPTER 1

The Erosion of our Political Foundation

• • •

"America will never be destroyed from the outside. If we falter and lose our freedoms, it will be because we destroyed ourselves."

ABRAHAM LINCOLN

WHEN AN OVERWHELMING MAJORITY OF people consider the highest cost in a nation's gross domestic product (GDP) to be damaged or very inefficient, there are serious problems. This is the case with America in 2016. Government is the largest-cost item in our GDP, and public opinion consistently ranks the political systems of our government as very poor or worse. Forced taxation has been elevated in today's marketplace as a means of distributing fairness and compassion through programs and ideas that are not fully desired by the public as a whole. This is not only unfair to many, but it is unsustainable for America to continue down this path.

Our founding fathers established America to separate from the motherland and focus on liberty and freedom. Their foundation was based strongly on individual self-reliance instead of reliance on government. This was a relatively new idea in 1776, one that helped set the groundwork and motivation for many great innovations and enterprises such as the computer, the light bulb, the telephone, the automobile, and so on. For over two hundred years, America established itself in the world as a truly exceptional nation built on a belief of self-reliance which helped us flourish with many economic and social advances that have benefited much of mankind throughout the world. A few of the key foundational basics of America that are under attack from within our shattered politics include:

Declaration of Independence, July 4, 1776 (Preamble)
We hold these truths to be self-evident, that all men are created equal, that they are endowed by their Creator with certain unalienable Rights that among these are Life, Liberty and the pursuit of Happiness.

That to secure these rights, Governments are instituted among Men, deriving their just powers from the consent of the governed, That whenever any Form of Government becomes destructive of these ends, it is the Right of the People to alter or to abolish it, and to institute new Government, laying its foundation on such principles and organizing its powers in such form, as to them shall seem most likely to affect their Safety and Happiness. Prudence, indeed, will dictate that Governments long established should not be changed for light and transient causes; and accordingly all experience hath shewn, that mankind are more disposed to suffer, while evils are sufferable, than to right themselves by abolishing the forms to which they are accustomed. But when a long train of abuses and usurpations, pursuing invariably the same Object evinces a design to reduce them under absolute Despotism, it is their right, it is their duty, to throw off such Government, and to provide new Guards for their future security.

Constitution, 1789 (Preamble)
We the People of the United States, in Order to form a more perfect Union, establish Justice, insure domestic Tranquility, provide for the common defense, promote the general Welfare, and secure the Blessings of Liberty to ourselves and our Posterity, do ordain and establish this Constitution for the United States of America.

Bill of Rights, created in 1789 and ratified in 1791

The Bill of Rights is the collective name for the first ten amendments to the United States Constitution. Proposed following the oftentimes bitter 1787–88 battle over ratification of the Constitution and crafted to address the objections by Anti-Federalists, the Bill of Rights amendments add certain safeguards of democracy—specific guarantees of personal freedoms and rights; clear limitations on the government's power in judicial and other proceedings; and explicit declarations that all powers not specifically delegated to congress by the constitution are reserved for the states or the people—to the constitution.

10th Amendment (Principles of Federalism)

The powers not delegated to the United States by the Constitution, nor prohibited by it to the States, are reserved to the States respectively, or to the people.

Self-reliance has deteriorated as Americans have become more dependent on government to help us, whether in good times or bad. The capitalist spirit of endless opportunities for all has devolved into "what handout is there for me?" in the next wave of government programs. Unfortunately, this has hurt America in many ways, and I believe that our founding fathers are tossing in their graves, wondering what happened to the land of the free and home of the brave. In many ways, America has lost its first love of independence.

America's shattered politics is ranked in many polls as the biggest challenge our country faces today. Therefore, we will take an inside look at our political system and the internal war going on to take the power away from citizens and place it into the hands of an ever-growing, unsustainable government that no longer serves the people first. When it comes to politics, there is often room for significant debate and differences of opinion, but when it comes to assessing whether or not our politicians genuinely represent the interests of the people, public sentiment is quite clear according to a June 15, 2015 story in Time Magazine which stated that "86% of Americans say they feel the political system does NOT serve the interests of the people."[2]

America's Declaration of Independence outlines a moral vision of a government—and that vision is crumbling before our eyes. My hope is to shine a light on the efforts going on within many political circles today to undo the self-reliance that America was founded on. This is being carried out by self-serving and corrupt politicians who are more interested in power than genuine public service. To those elected officials who humbly serve the public good with pure and honest motives, I say thank you, and please keep up those efforts. Those who are in the game of politics for other selfish motives should remember that America has a rich history of overcoming big problems, and the citizens of our nation will be watching more closely in time ahead to make sure they serve their constituents first.

Some of the key points from this chapter are as follows:

- Government is America's largest-cost item in our GDP, and rated as one of our biggest problems by most Americans.
- America was uniquely founded based on individual self-reliance, not reliance on government.
- The Declaration of Independence is a key foundational statement of our nation's identity.
- The Constitution, Bill of Rights and the 10th Amendment are also key principles to America's identity.
- The individual self-reliant nation of America has severely eroded as government takes further control over a rapidly increasing number of frustrated citizens.

"Our government has become too responsive to trivial or ephemeral concerns, often at the expense of more important concerns or an erosion of our liberty, and it has made policy priorities more

*dependent on where TV journalists happen to point their cameras…
As a nation we have lost our sense of tragedy, a recognition that bad
things happen to good people. A nation that expects the government
to prevent churches from burning, to control the price of bread
or gasoline, to secure every job, and to find some villain for every
dramatic accident, risks an even larger loss of life and liberty."*

WILLIAM A. NISKANEN

CHAPTER 2

We, The People, Have Lost Our Government to the Political Elite

• • •

Why do we keep asking politicians to solve complex problems
when we have such little respect for their profession?

AN OVERWHELMING MAJORITY OF AMERICAN citizens believe that our politicians have failed us and is the largest problem or one of the largest problems facing us today. We will dive into a myriad of problems associated with our shattered politics, but any honest assessment of the failure of the American political system must begin with an examination of the voters who elect these politicians into office in the first place. It is time to set the record straight by identifying the people at fault for this collapse: it is us, the American people. Many people attempt to shrug off this responsibility by blaming uneducated voters or politicians from other districts, but, as a nation, we must look at the citizens who continue to elect a number of incompetent politicians who are destroying our nation from within. The great news is that Americans have the power to be the solution to the problems we face; conversely, we can also continue to be the problem instead of the solution if we take no action.

It is important for all concerned citizens to look in the mirror and realize that far too many of us are asking our elected officials to solve more and more problems. In a sense, we have given up the responsibility of overseeing our government by giving politicians more opportunity to solve problems that American citizens used to solve by themselves. In response, many power-hungry elected officials have willingly served this ever-expanding service industry by striving to satisfy the growing demands of its customers. The problem becomes an ever-expanding role of government in attempting to solve more and more problems, too often with mediocre results.

As we continue giving politicians more power to dictate public policy and programs, even though we far too often do not like the results achieved or the means by which they are achieved, we expand the dynamics of the political system that was originally intended to serve us, not control us. That which gets rewarded, gets repeated, and politicians are no different from others in a free market in that they pursue opportunities where power and the dollar reside. Unfortunately, we are now in a time when too many politicians take actions that bring themselves power or large paychecks while they harm the jurisdiction that they were elected to govern and serve. For example, Congress requires citizens to procure healthcare while excluding itself from that same requirement.

The irony of this power struggle between citizens and politicians is that the American political system was effectively designed to limit the power of politicians.

The founding fathers viewed government as a necessary evil to be guarded against as much as possible. For many decades, individuals who would serve in this profession were honorable statesmen who earned the respect of the public by adhering to strong virtues and a commitment to preserving our nation. Fast forward to the twentieth century, when modern thought evolved into a new view of government as an "engine of good" and an instrument to solve all manners of social problems.[3] Now in the twenty-first century, in a world that is becoming more and more specialized each day, it is an interesting paradox that our citizens are asking elected officials (generalist administrators/leaders) to solve more complex problems. It is akin to asking a general doctor to do one's hip replacement, a home builder to fix physical ailments, or accountants to provide sound legal advice. The end results are usually not good.

These foundational principles of America were boldly put in place to set our governing system apart from virtually all others in that individuals—not the government—were empowered with freedom and the opportunity to pursue happiness. The founding fathers knew from history that, unchecked, the uncontrollable quest for power by politicians could result in taking over the resources of the people being governed. In 2016, it is very easy to say that politicians have more power than the people they represent as "We, the People" have had our voices virtually shut down by politicians.

It is interesting that America has historically been known as a beacon of liberty around the world, yet, the United States has had one of the lowest levels of electoral participation in the world, ranking a lowly 31 out of 34 developed countries for which data exists on voter turnout.[4] The American people are tired of bad politics, yet we continue to make the problem worse by not voting and allowing the political elite to gain more control over the citizenship. Below is a summary of some of the main reasons people give for wanting to be less involved in their political process.

- Frustration—Many have given up trying to do their part to fix a system that they view as "unfixable."
- A disconnect between the system and citizens—There is a growing separation between the political elites and real-world citizens.
- Difference in values—Families and working-class citizens feel more alienated after years of empty promises made by self-serving politicians.
- Less of a priority—There is an increasing preference to avoid politics and spend time on other priorities such as work, family, and hobbies.

- Apathy—A growing number of citizens who would rather watch reality T.V. than pay attention to the world around them since there is a belief that their voice does not matter anyway.
- Political correctness—Citizens are becoming too intimidated to speak out against special interest groups that have perceived opposing views.
- Consumerism—A culture of instant gratification consumers that believe that their own immediate desires are more important than planning for future generations.

Two primary groups of people were intended to govern in America: citizens and their elected representatives (politicians). As government grew, so has the role of other secondary groups of influence such as lobbyists and a wide range of special-interest groups. These special-interest groups have brought forward many unique issues that are a blend of societal and governmental issues, and the mixing of these two driving forces has greatly expanded the role of government in America. Society is intended to be made up of like-minded groups who care for our individual well-being, while government's role is to restrain other groups from infringing on those societal rights. As Thomas Paine states in *Common Sense, Rights of Man*, this can be dangerous: "Society is produced by our wants and government by our wickedness—the former promotes our happiness by uniting our affections while the later negatively by restraining our vices. Society in every state is a blessing, but government in its best state is but a necessary evil; in its worst state an intolerable one."[5]

When one looks at the vast number of impure motives that overtly guide the decision-making process of many of our elected officials, it is easy to understand the frustrations of the voter. Special-interest groups have taken over more of the political discourse and squeezed out the voice of many hardworking citizens who prefer to preserve a nation focused on the core foundational principles of liberty and freedom. When constituents become more apathetic, the number of citizens holding these politicians accountable dwindles and the downward spiral of our shattered politics continues to worsen with less accountability.

When more specialized interest groups, as well as general citizenship, ask for more from their elected officials who are willing to overstep their responsibilities to please their constituents, we create a significant "confidence gap." According to Gallup polls, this gap has been getting significantly worse in recent decades.[6] America's tolerance for more empty or misleading political promises is waning very thin.

Frustrations are growing high in America as we watch self-reliance losing control to politicians whom we do not respect. In addition, the political system that was intended to be local has been taken over by a federal government that makes it more difficult to pinpoint responsibility. That is the sad state of our nation, but it's not too hard to grasp how it happened when one looks at the large gap between voters and their elected officials, who break promises to fix any of the ongoing problems facing the constituents. When voter apathy increases among average Americans, special-interest groups tend to take over more political affairs, thus further influencing general public opinion regarding unique problems facing our nation rather than the day-to-day burdens facing the normal American family. Unfortunately, specialized political problem solving has created more injustices in our current culture, further exacerbating many of our social problems and alienating many frustrated voters.

Another frightening reason the average American citizen is being turned off by politics is the increasingly excessive use of intimidation by arrogant politicians who are telling us to shut up and not allowing us to voice our concerns since the politicians supposedly know what's best for their people. As Harry S. Truman once said, "When even one American— who has done nothing wrong—is forced by fear to shut his mind and close his mouth, then all Americans are in peril."

Perhaps the strongest example showing that citizens are subservient to political elites (a definition of *"political elite"* is provided in Section 14 of this book, under Revised Political Speak) is when they are blatantly told to shut up, and their input is not allowed. Personally, I find it encouraging when citizens take time out of their busy schedules to embrace their First Amendment right and voice concerns about their government since that is the way a free society should work. However, we know of too many instances in America today when political elites shut down public input, and this is very dangerous to any nation that values freedom. Citizens know that nothing will ever change for the better if we shut up and go away, but there are far too many governmental organizations that have gotten away with telling citizens to do just that, "Go away; your voice does not matter here." I know that there are numerous examples across the nation of arrogant public officials who deliberately refuse public comment or input on public decisions, and one example I'll share is taken verbatim from my local paper on August 23, 2012.

Isanti-Chisago County Star

Constituents' right to speak causes disagreement

Tiffany Kafer | Posted Aug 23, 2012

After yet another attempt of the public to speak during the Isanti County Board meeting, one commissioner showed his disapproval voting not to approve the agenda.

During the Aug. 15 meeting of the board, Commissioner Alan Duff raised questions over whether or not there had been interest expressed by the public to speak to the board.

"The administrator has the authority to set the agenda," explained Chair George Larson. "If what they [constituents] have to offer comes in the

realms of what he [Isanti County Administrator Kevin VanHooser] thinks is the best for the county, then he has the authority to put it on the agenda."

"In our last meeting it was mentioned, you [Larson] mentioned that if a person had something to say to go through our administrator, and if that process has been done, I think that we should," Duff began to state, but was interrupted by Larson saying, "If they have a request that pertains to pertinent county business, then I think that it is up to his [VanHooser's] discretion to do that."

Attention was then turned to County Attorney Jeff Edblad for a legal standpoint.

"I concur with the chair that as far as the agenda is set, the practice has always been the administrator receives the requests, the administrator then adds items to the agenda that are within his discretion reflecting on county business, and it's the chair that controls the agenda for the meetings," said Edblad.

"The city of Cambridge and the city of Isanti, Chisago County and many other towns allow public input," explained Duff. "And I think that we should."

"I think this is something that we have to decide, and I think that at our annual meeting in January, this will probably be set up and we will probably have a list of things at that time that we will decide on," explained Larson. "At this time, we don't have that and it is up to the discretion of our administrator."

Commissioner Susan Morris moved to approve the agenda, which was seconded by Commissioner Mike Warring. The motion passed 4-1 with Duff voting no.[7]

Concerned citizens must make every legal effort to express concerns with their elected officials or far too many will end up wondering why our taxes keep going up while the problems get worse.

Some of the key points in this chapter include the following:

- The US political system was designed for us to be in charge, but with this privilege comes responsibility, which we have given away to the political elite.
- The US political system was designed with an emphasis of governing at the local level, but that has now been taken over by the federal government, which further distances the voters from the issues.
- America's confidence in our current political system suffers due to an overload of empty promises and failed results.
- Discouraged voters are walking away from the process out of frustration, and more shenanigans are being done behind our backs with a lower percentage of citizens watching.
- There are a growing number of politicians who do not listen to or respect us and want us to stay away from their elite insider group.
- Limited government has been overtaken by overwhelming societal wants that are fiscally unsustainable.
- The United States is crumbling from within, and most people sense it.

"The price of apathy towards public affairs is to be ruled by evil men."

PLATO

CHAPTER 3

Politicians Eager to Fix All
of "Your" Problems

• • •

"No one will really understand politics until they understand that
politicians are not trying to solve our problems. They are trying to
solve their own problems—of which getting elected and re-elected are
number one and number two. Whatever is number three is far behind."

THOMAS SOWELL

ELECTION CAMPAIGNS TO INCREASE CANDIDATES' political power have
become a multi-billion-dollar industry fueled by those wanting the
stage for fixing our social problems and an eager constituency willing
to pay them for that privilege. In 2012, America spent approximately $6
billion on political campaigns for federal candidates.[8] Beyond presidential and congressional races, Americans also spent billions of dollars
on state and local races. The fuel for those seeking public office has
become an expensive affair, and the funding of this industry has grown
more than that for most other industries or other economic trends.
Not only are we asking politicians to solve more of our problems, but
we are also investing significantly more of our money to fund our fa-
vorites (though it's hard to say "favorite" when most politicians are not
respected).

Politicians consistently rank in Gallop polls as one of the least respected and trusted professions in America. In late 2013, three of the four lowest-respected professions were directly related to politicians (state-elected officials, congress members, and lobbyists); the other was car salespeople.[9] Yet in spite of our low respect for members of this profession, they are far too often the group we go to first to solve our social problems. The results can be dangerous as we place our hopes on fixing problems with a group that we do not respect, is often found to be disingenuous or even outright untruthful, and far too often are inexperienced problem solvers tackling issues beyond both their abilities and authority within the elected office they serve. Elected office in the United States was designed to be a temporary and honorable public service, not a career profession.

The same Gallup poll found nurses, pharmacists, grade-school teachers, medical doctors, and military officers to be the five most honest and ethical professions. These respected professionals are generally those who serve or protect others while adhering to strict professional codes and guidelines in how they conduct their business. There is a great contrast in the qualities that comprise the respected professions and the disrespected ones, and these rankings obviously change over time. But why are politicians and those with related professions ranked so low in our current day?

Politicians have become akin to salesmen, selling products and services that are requested by their constituents. Similar to America's low levels of respect for used-car salesmen, Americans often view politicians as having little to no ethical virtues, hence their extremely low respect levels across the United States. It is obvious that their ability to share only some of the entire truth has caught up with this position. Politicians are selling lots of lemons, and we need better answers from better experts and leaders who care more about the welfare of our nation/community than they do about personal payback to those investing in their power. Unfortunately, politicians have perfected the art of selling hope while losing focus on reality. Too many of them love to prey on the weaknesses of people rather than identify ways to revive the American dream of endless opportunities for all. They claim they can fix all your problems but fail to reveal the real cost of that promise.

Self-serving politicians are enthusiastically eager to accept more power, while the genuine purity of public service gets left behind. Unfortunately for America, power-hungry politicians rule over true servant leaders, and this has caused great dysfunction within many political circles. Many of us have probably even observed new politicians who start off with good intentions, but once within the system, they cave into the political power game as that is usually their only way to stay in control. In sum, more power is gained within the current political system through leveraging relationships and resources to expand government services for constituents, regardless of the costs to the citizens.

Elected officials seeking to boost their egos or make political tradeoffs to help climb the political ladder often make empty promises or deliver short-term answers that cause negative long-term results. Paybacks to powerful groups may appease some, but they can endanger the welfare of the general citizenship. For example, I'm reminded of a former commissioner who voted for a less-qualified administrator because it would allow him/her to gain other political powers, even though the person readily admitted that this political choice was not in the best interest of the citizens s/he represented. This is political decision-making that damages our government as the politician gains political power while constituents lose public value.

The power sought by politicians only gets exasperated when one looks at the close interdependence among different layers of government. City officials who have special connections or abilities to convince county officials to reward them with more county funds often get rewarded with political wins from voters eager to reallocate more funds to their areas. The same goes for state officials with connections to federal officials, and by the time one gets to the federal level, those who bring home the most bacon usually win the prize of being elected to office. Along the way, the real wants and needs of the constituents get left behind as the long trail of paybacks allows for little public service or truly providing effective solutions that do not involve more government programs.

Far too many politicians have ended up picking winners and losers in the game of forced taxation instead of promoting equality and fairness for all citizens. Unfortunately, hardworking Americans have suffered as elected officials are more interested in forming allegiances with other elected officials to support their biased pet projects or groups of friends instead of doing what is best for the whole of the public good. The end result is that politicians then become greedy, looking for more sources of revenue instead of considering tax breaks or improving services for their constituents.

The ambition to gain political power never ends as ego-driven politicians strive to manage our tax dollars, though they often fail at managing their own resources in a respectable manner. I knew one politician who admitted to stealing public dollars while in office who later said s/he was having financial problems at home. We can all have empathy for someone going through hard times, but does that give the politician the right to steal from the public trough? This certainly also brings up another question: if an elected official cannot adequately manage his or her own finances, why should the tax payer entrust him or her to manage the taxes within his or her control?

When the public eye is off them, politicians tend to do more deceitful things. Isn't it sad when politicians make so many promises before an election then seem to forget public service the day after they win their campaigns? During 2012, my last year in elected office, we had set the 2013 budget, as required by state statute, in mid-December. This budget was established with no discussion about any raises for county board members; in fact, holding commissioners' salaries in check was a campaign promise made by all the candidates before the elections. My last meeting was a special meeting on December 26, the day after Christmas, when others on the board proposed giving them- selves raises.[10] This raise passed on a 4–1 vote; I objected, stating that the raise was not in the budget and could only be paid for through more taxes since the original budget did not allocate for it. With actions like this, it becomes rather easy to see why public trust in elected officials is so low and why public budgets are too often mismanaged. One radio station voted Isanti County "jerk of the week" for this self-serving ac- tion, but, unfortunately, actions like this happen way too often in far too many political circles.

A lack of transparency only increases the motivation for some to pursue public office as many seek elected offices to serve their own egos and other motives that very rarely ever effectively solve real problems. They may want to help fix a problem but only through use of resources coerced or forced into action. I found it amazing how little honest debate takes place among elected officials when the public is not watching. Unfortunately, the discussions I observed over possible solutions to government priorities too often revolved around paying off special friends or supporters more than what would benefit the citizens most (or cost them the least amount of forced taxation).

Some pursue politics since it can pay more than other more difficult or riskier jobs. For example, many local politicians are paid far more than military reservists/national guard members or other part-time profes- sions. Far too many think, with history on their side to support them that political power will allow them to get away with more in legal circles. Unfortunately, most of us know stories of elected officials using their con- nections within legal offices to conceal violations such as driving while under the influence (DUI).

With such a horrible reputation, it is no wonder that many successful people have no interest in entering the political arena. The reality is that it is a profession that offers minimal job satisfaction, costs a large investment of time and dollars to enter, and has an ever-present pressure to bend the rules of common sense and moral guidance. There are certainly many who seek elected office for power, money, or other self-serving interests; however, there also are a large number of well-intentioned Americans, especially in recent years, who seek to serve in elected office with genuine interest in making their areas better. Unfortunately, many of these individuals are getting eaten up within the big political machine that is in power and does not want to welcome new perspectives that serve constituents in a purer manner.

This takes us to the fundamental question of just which qualities are embodied by a typical politician in the twenty-first century. Obviously, there are many variables to this question, but below is a summary of some of the attributes that are often *not* needed in politicians but are frequently required in other professions.

- educational requirements (most professional jobs require a degree)
- budgeting experience (though that is the fundamental job of a politician)
- business or notable civic accomplishments
- notable discipline training (such as military service)
- accountability as well as financial or personal responsibilities
- specific commitments to sacrifice (such as military or police service)
- commitment to any higher power or principles (such as clergy or teachers)
- certifications or ethical standards to abide by

In general, one can quickly recognize that though politicians require votes to hold and maintain office, they otherwise have very few prerequisites for the position that are so common among other professions. In some ways, this is good as it allows an opportunity for public service for most citizens, but it is also dangerous as lesser-qualified politicians may be prone to blending into the shattered political system or are too fixated on just a few issues instead of true governance. In contrast, the skills they generally do have often include:

* personal desire for power, inflated ego, or high income
* willingness to campaign for the position, often including smearing an opponent with or without any factual basis
* communication skills with a focus on showing compassion to their current audience even though those promises may hurt others not in that crowd
* ability to persuade voters that they can help them (often with minimal connection to the actual role of the office being sought)
* ability to raise funds through power groups outside of the general citizenry (thus alliances are already built into decision-making processes)

Power corrupts, and any system that empowers individuals to spend other people's money, as well as allowing them to grant favors to themselves and their supporters with that money, is prime breeding territory for corruption. Once in office, politicians become especially dangerous when they carry the force of law and are often making these laws in a manner that benefits their own self-interests to the detriment of the constituents they supposedly represent. Americans keep asking politicians to solve more problems; our spending to help candidates get in power to address those questions keeps increasing, and so the ever-evolving growth of government continues to spiral out of control while the taxpayers suffer. At some point, virtually every American will need to stop and ask, "How can we make sure politicians become accountable for their actions similar to the way we ask other professions to be accountable for their actions?"

Some of the key points from this chapter are as follow:

* The dollar amount spent on political campaigns is astronomical.
* Politicians are selling us a lot of false promises, and they, along with related professionals such as lobbyists, are some of the least-respected individuals in America today.
* Once politicians are in the system, their campaign promises associated with public service often give way to protecting their power and paying back special friends.
* Political mischief increases when public awareness decreases.
* Many of the political elite believe they are above the law and that they are entitled to compensation and privileges beyond the realities of the marketplace.

"Government's first duty is to protect the people, not run their lives."

RONALD REAGAN

CHAPTER 4

How Much Government Is Enough?

• • •

"It was self-serving politicians who convinced recent generations
of Americans that we could all stand in a circle with our
hands in each other's pockets and somehow get rich."

PAUL HARVEY

OVERVIEW OF GOVERNMENT

FOR THE FIRST TWO HUNDRED years of America's remarkable history, the aggregate burden of government was below 10 percent of our gross domestic product (GDP). This low cost to the average producer in America allowed the nation to grow in a way that was consistent with the beliefs of its founders. The government's role was generally limited to national defense, policing, and administration and this philosophy helped foster economic expansion as never seen before in the history of the world.

The founding fathers recognized that excessive government could ruin any free society and that greed and gluttony would result in over-spending and the possible end of any nation that values the rights of the individual more than government's right to rule over its people. Absolute power with forced taxation to pay for out-of-control spending is danger-ous to a free society, and that is exactly what is happening before our very eyes in America today as taxation—including federal, state, and local levels—now represents about 40 percent of our GDP.

For many years, the American dream included a positive look toward the future, but that future is now in jeopardy as we struggle to pay back our debts for our fiscal excesses. To put it bluntly, the future sustainability of America is dependent on living within our means. Just like with family and business budgets, borrowing can help us purchase important items such as homes, vehicles, and capital equipment; however, when we fail to repay our debts, we become dependent on others, and that is dangerous as well as unfair to future generations to inherit this debt so that we can live beyond our means today. It is difficult to write the national debt of America in ink as it increases so quickly, but the last count was $19 trillion and still rapidly growing. A government that recklessly spends more than what is taken in is arguably endangering its national security.

I find it discouraging that while businesses constantly evaluate how to maintain profitability and sustainability in a competitive marketplace, these sustainable concepts are virtually unheard of in many public circles. But why should politicians concern themselves with managing a fiscally responsible government when the people continue to be passive in fighting for accountability for their hard-earned tax dollars? As Ronald Reagan once said, "The closest thing to eternal life in America is a government program."

To give a historical context, in 1784, Patrick Henry, with the initial support of George Washington and John Marshal, introduced a bill in the Virginia House of Delegates authorizing "a moderate tax or contribution annually for the support of the Christian religion."[11] This effort was quickly shot down. That kind of political effort today would be unheard of as separation of church and state is clearly in the mind-set of most Americans. Yet we so often undertake a similar effort by taxing (forcing payment from) constituents and then handing over the money to nonprofits or other social organizations who ask for help.

Though most agree that tax funds would never be given to any religious organization in modern-day America, most are amazed at just how much money is collected via the force of taxation so that politicians can give to their favorite charities. These elected officials then often serve on these charitable boards. When did America's government take over the job of forcing us to pay for charitable efforts that benefit the politician more than the constituents? There are many worthy charities out there, but shouldn't that support come freely from people who want to help that cause instead of through forced taxation?

Thomas Jefferson's statement from the eighteenth century is relevant today: "most bad government results from too much government." That can also be applied to businesses that operate with too much overhead. We must begin by stating just how much government is out there for the average citizen in America. Obviously, the details vary from locale to locale, but most people are stunned when they realize just how many layers of government have a taxing authority over them. Most people I speak with believe that their taxes are too high, but few realize just how many different taxing authorities have a legal right to tax them for many nonessential services. The following is a typical overview of the layers of government to which residents pay taxes and a broad range of their associated costs to the taxpayer:

* federal (15–25 percent)
* state (4–7 percent)
* regional/multijurisdictional (0–5 percent)
* county (3–10 percent)
* city or township (1–5 percent)
* watershed (0–2 percent)
* lake districts

* housing agencies
* libraries
* economic development authorities/districts

Smaller governmental bodies such as cities or townships often become constant lobbyists in that they often ask their higher levels of government for more subsidies, distribution, and so on. Look at the distribution of federal funds to the various states, and you basically have full-time lobbyists/ politicians fighting for money to return to their districts. This same thing happens in most states with trickle-down redistribution mechanisms. Wouldn't it be much more effective if each organization focused on its own specific issues? But that simply is not happening as lobbying for redistribution of tax dollars has become a full-time job, replacing local problem solving as a key task for many of our state and local elected officials.

This is not a federal government problem but, rather, an overall problem of abuse of power by elected officials at every level of government. Though there are obviously many exceptions, I have generally found that the levels of government closest to the constituents they serve <u>and</u> those watched by their constituents are best run. However, there are so many layers and levels of government that most people are not even aware of, so proper monitoring or watchdog efforts can be overwhelming for the average hardworking person. As James Madison once said, "Redistribution and pork barrel spending attracts and corrupts both voters and politicians alike."[12]

Before we review the three primary governing bodies (federal, state, and local), please note that there are many taxing tools used by government, including income tax, payroll tax, property tax, sales tax, import tax, estate tax, gifts tax, and many other local user fees and local specialized taxes. So many Americans grumble around April 15 as they see their tax burdens in black and white. But remember that taxes are paid on a daily basis to numerous taxing authorities.

Let us now review some of the fundamental basics of the three key levels of government in America: federal, state, and local.

Federal Level

"Congress is like two drunks arguing the bar bill on the Titanic."

Young Americans for Liberty

The establishment of the United States of America included an emphasis on taxation to be determined at each respective state level of government. This would help ensure taxation at a more local of government where citizens could have a more direct impact on the priorities that are relevant to their specific jurisdiction. However, this has not happened as the federal government accounts for over half (55 percent) of the overall taxation in America today. Federal taxation has gotten out of hand, creating a serious disconnect between the US heartland and Washington, DC.

The US debt is $19 trillion and is growing by more than $2 billion each day. These numbers seem very large, and, indeed, they are, but when one personalizes it, these numbers become much more real and alarming. The average debt for our 321 million residents is over fifty-six thousand dollars per person. That is the "gift" our children are inheriting from our government, and increasing this debt amount is simply unsustainable. How did we get into this mess? There are certainly many reasons, but at the heart of the matter is a federal government that has not even established a budget in many years. One would think that would be the fundamental job of Congress, but it simply has not been undertaken in quite some time.

Half of US federal expenditures are for social services such as Social Security and Medicare. I will not spend a lot of time debating this level of public taxation, but, needless to say, these public-subsistence programs are unsustainable in their current forms. Though it is frustrating for our aging population to recognize that their years of paying into Social Security may not return as good a value as in past years, the example of Social Security running out of sustainable funding is a great illustration of our shattered politics as earmarked social-service funds were "borrowed" for other political purposes.

One federal-budget line item that needs to be seriously addressed is the redistribution of federal taxes to states since this dangerous trail of taxation has built-in mechanisms that promote more government in a manner that is unsustainable and exacerbates our overall problem. Redistribution of taxes also promotes more lobbying and unfairness in use of our tax dollars. An out-of-control federal government forces excessive tax levels, skims our tax dollars off the top for managing these funds, and then redistributes them to state and local governmental agencies, usually with numerous strings attached as to how they can spend these funds. In addition, this approach is also frustrating for taxpayers, who are further removed from recognizing the value of their tax money.

It can be very difficult to implement quality improvements within large bureaucratic organizations. To help give an illustration of how difficult it can be to improve large organizations and how excessive bureaucracy can hurt an organization, the following are a couple of examples of the struggles associated with making effective changes within larger bureaucracies in the United States in recent years.

* Veterans Affairs (VA): The VA is one of the largest organizations in the world, and I will vouch as a veteran that there are many fantastic workers there; however, the continuous cover-ups of failed programs in recent years by bureaucrats that have resulted in tragic deaths and serious illnesses of too many military veterans should be unacceptable to a free society and needs to be overhauled as soon as possible. When the end result is *zero* terminations and

only lip-service accountability for many serious wrongdoings, the status quo of mediocrity is most likely to continue.

* Social Security: Americans entrust a part of their incomes toward a federal government retirement program that is supposed to at least partially help retired workers; however, the trustee of our funds has opened up the vault for other "important" services, and Social Security funds may not be available for future generations.
* Department of Defense: Perhaps the saddest commentary on the infamous 1980s naval aircraft $659-per-ashtray procurement story was not about the greedy contractors or incompetent military officers who allowed this to happen but that there were no significant systemic changes to the $100-billion-a-year military procurement system.

Before starting an argument that businesses should be taxed more, keep in mind that America's corporate tax rate is already one of the highest in the world.[13] Higher taxes make it even more difficult for small business to succeed in a nation filled with many great entrepreneurs who have the energy, passion, and creativity to bring many more new ideas to fruition if they are allowed to in an open and competitive marketplace not constrained by excessive tax burdens.

STATE LEVEL

Overall, state government represents approximately 25 percent of the typical overall tax burden for the average American. The average state tax on citizens in 2015 was approximately fifty-five hundred dollars per person (this is an approximate amount based on various public reports and generally includes local taxes as well). This amount fluctuates by state, with Alaska's tax the lowest at about $3000 per person to the highest rate of about $7500 in Illinois. In general, state taxes are increasing, and all but five states now have a sales tax.[14]

In Minnesota, for example, the state biennium budget has increased from approximately $30 billion to $40 billion in the past five years.[15] To help illustrate how out of control taxation has gotten here, the State of Minnesota has over twenty-five special taxing districts within its overall budget. This list was sent to me by a state legislator who eagerly admitted that it was excessive. When I reviewed these items with concerned citizens, the most common response was, "Why am I paying taxes for areas so far away or for issues that do not impact me in my place of living or work?" This general concept continues to show that a primary frustration among taxpayers is paying for projects and services where they see or feel minimal benefits.

LOCAL LEVEL
Local government represents approximately 20 percent of the overall tax burden for the average American. However, do not let that fool you as this amount can be much higher in some locales throughout the country. As an example of excessive local government, our property taxes on our homes represent over one quarter of our monthly principal/interest/taxes/insurance (PITI) payment. If you own a home and pay property taxes, take a look at your house payment details and determine your tax burden associated with your local government.

One state where local government has arguably gotten most out of control is Illinois. In his article *"Why Is Illinois So Corrupt?,"* Shane Tritsch writes that as of 2010, Illinois had almost seven thousand separate local-level governmental organizations—far more than any other state.[16] He explains that this excessive number of local governing bodies resulted from a state constitution that was in effect from 1870 to 1970 that limited the amount of debt that counties and municipalities could carry and taxes they could levy. When cities needed to fund improvements, they got around those constraints by creating new units of government with the capacity to borrow. As is pointed out in the article, most of these local governmental bodies have budgets to protect and authority to wield, making it very hard for citizens to stay on top of it all, and this creates many opportunities for patronage as well as small of islands of corruption. This brings up three significant problems:

1) Politicians can be creative in working around limits and develop- ing spinoff political bodies that grow government.
2) Citizens' monitoring of political corruption can be overwhelming with the large number of public entities in place.
3) Taking away those added layers of government is virtually impos- sible without a strong, coordinated effort by concerned citizens.

Cities and towns are generally most efficient as constituents work most directly with them. However, local government includes numerous other political entities that are often unknown or too distant for constituents to watch in a productive manner. This is where political favors can be had by political insiders who promise local nonprofit organizations financial as- sistance for political contributions. For example, when I was on the Isanti County Board, approximately $175,000 out of our $30-million budget was earmarked for charitable organizations. Should our government really be using forced taxation to support charitable organizations?

As mentioned before, the trickling down of funds from the federal and state levels to local government is significant. For example, our local Isanti County budget increased from $38 to $42 million between 2015 and 2016, an increase of more than 10 percent at a time when inflation was closer to 2 or 3 percent. Out of this $42-million budget, nearly 40 percent of the revenues are received from federal and state revenues, including fed- eral intergovernmental payout ($6.7 million) and state intergovernmental handouts ($12 million).[17]

This redistribution of tax dollars from places far away is contributing mightily to our problem. When the federal government taxes one hundred dollars from someone in, say, Minnesota, they keep ten dollars in DC as an administration fee/service, and then they decide to give ninety dollars to a complete stranger in Oregon. The costs and benefits are impossible to identify as the long trail of trickle-down tax dollars changes hands and the programs and policies it supports loses its intended value or purpose.

Summary about Your Taxes

Some of the key points from this chapter are as follow:

- There are three primary taxing levels—federal, state, and local—though there are many sublevels underneath each of these primary levels.
- There are numerous taxing mechanisms beyond income and sales taxes.
- The US Constitution was founded on a limited federal government, but in 2016, about 55 percent of our overall tax burden is paid to the federal government, 25 percent to state government, and 20 percent to local government.
- The current debt of the US federal government is over $19 trillion and continues to grow rapidly.
- Our current $19-trillion debt equates to a fifty-six-thousand-dollar inherited liability for every American woman, man, and child.
- There is a significant transfer of tax dollars from the federal government to the state and local levels of government, making it difficult to identify the true value or cost of many governmental programs and services.
- The government confiscates tax dollars to support numerous charities at many levels of government.

The federal GAO office published the following in 2009 (please note that the situation is much worse now than it was then): "According to the Government Accountability Office (GAO), the US is on a fiscally *unsustainable path* because of projected future increases in Medicare and Social Security spending, and that politicians and the electorate have been *unwilling* to change this path."

CHAPTER 5

Deferring Responsibility via the Political Blame Game

• • •

When was the last time you heard a politician accept responsibility, especially during campaign season?

THE POLITICAL SYSTEM IS SHATTERED, and finding someone to accept responsibility for this failure is nearly impossible. At virtually every level of political service, there is a major lack of true leadership and stewardship by responsible leaders who will accept responsibility for shortcomings within their authority. The American people are tired of the irresponsible behavior of our politicians, and this chapter will take a brief look at three parts of the problem:

- The blame game—unfortunately, a skill that has been perfected by far too many politicians
- Backroom deals—the debate over public value is not done in public as transparency has essentially vanished in many public circles
- Lack of honest debate—which has been replaced with childish name-calling

The Blame Game

Isn't it sad that one of the best skills offered by far too many politicians is a unique ability to escape responsibility for making poor decisions?

We all know how politicians love to blame others, especially their opponents, for all the problems facing their political jurisdictions. But isn't this approach getting old? When will politics attract true leaders who want to fix problems and stop blaming others? America eagerly awaits this transition, but until that happens, we will continue to be bombarded with television commercials that slam others while no real progress is made to solve increasingly dangerous problems in our nation.

The blame game is an interesting paradox to modern-day business, where capitalistic ideas generally thrive when business leaders create valuable commodities or services that are wanted in the marketplace. Notice that business leaders focus on finding solutions to marketplace conditions, whereas far too many politicians focus on blaming others for their problems. In business, if a solution is deemed to be too expensive, unknown, or of poor quality, consumers will not pay the price; however, in politics, we continue to pay a high price to watch politicians bash each other with no quality solutions in sight. So why do politicians continue to bash each other? The answer is that it is easier to sell negativity or conflict than it is to provide a clear, simple and legitimate solution in today's fast-paced world that wants quick answers to very challenging problems. With this mentality, it is easy to see why many people end up voting for the lesser of two evils.

Not only are many Americans getting tired of the old blame game by politicians, but there is a true cost that is paid when the focus is blaming rather than problem solving.

Instead of honest assessments about what is or is not working or is of real value, too many political decisions are based on protecting images and finding ways to present answers in a manner that is palatable to constituents but is not truly effective in reality. Self-survival and self-promotion guide far too many public decisions, but they are not in the best interests of the constituents. The following are some of the primary negative results and dysfunction caused by a system that has perfected the craft of blaming others:

- It emphasizes problems or temporary solutions instead of viable and sustainable solutions that can be measured for accountability.
- Fixing the issue becomes secondary to destroying the person or the other political party.
- There is an increase of fear, negativity, and distance between the citizen and the political elite.
- It reduces the morale of public employees who have minimal respect for their elected representatives yet cannot speak out against their failures.
- It lowers the interest level of many good-hearted Americans to enter the political arena with fresh ideas.

At the heart of the blame game at the national level is the constant bickering between the two main political parties. Virtually every American I know is tired of this never-ending battle of blaming the other, and it has resulted in a growing appetite for different political options that are more focused on problem solving rather than blaming. Avoiding any form of political accountability will continue to exacerbate the ongoing demise of our nation.

Beyond the nonstop blame game that we are used to seeing with politicians at the federal level, there are also seemingly innocent forms of neglecting responsibility for public funds that are just as dangerous. Specifically, there are some elected officials who wrongly believe that it is the responsibility of their public employees to set taxing policy. It is very irresponsible and dangerous for any elected official to neglect responsibility for establishing taxation levels and deflecting this responsibility to staff. If public employees are setting our tax levy, then why do we even need elected officials? Who is representing the taxpayer? This is akin to employees setting company budgets (it may sound like a good idea for some of the employees, but it generally will become unsustainable at some point in time). We need elected officials who recognize that their job is to set budgets, establish sustainable and defendable tax levels, and not delegate this responsibility to their staff, who will be more than willing to increase your taxes to pay their own salaries. Elected officials are the medium between the supplier (their staff) and their consumer (the public), and they should manage both sides of this equation with fairness for all concerned, not show any bias toward the staff that work for them.

This is an important factor in why America has shattered politics as too many elected officials give more weight to serving their internal partners (benefiting receivers such as public employees) instead of the hardworking constituents that they are elected to serve (payers). Until the citizenship speaks as loudly as the recipients of the system, elected officials will continue to underrepresent the citizens they are elected to serve.

BACKROOM DEALS HAVE REPLACED PUBLIC SERVICE

Do you ever feel like public decisions are mostly made in private?

Unfortunately, far too little public service is conducted by politicians in a manner that is truly serving the public as a whole. Transparency has given way to cutting deals behind closed doors so that public scrutiny does not get in the way of decision-making deals. For security-related or human-resource-related items, I can understand the need for confidentiality within a public organization, but backroom deals have overtaken way too much of the public decision-making process for public bodies that were originally intended to serve a public good.

Based on my experience, I would estimate that over half of genuine political discourse and decision-making takes place away from the public eye. Even though there are rules against collusion at most levels of government, it takes place far too often. I believe that American politics was intended to be a form of problem solving in front of the constituents impacted by the decisions made. This style of governance would lead to genuine, honest, open debate, which can lead to bringing many perspectives together and combining them into the most optimal result for the group at large.

With all the problems going on at Isanti County while I served on that board, I had many constituents ask if they could hear or watch our meetings as the stories were often too unbelievable for many to comprehend when they could only hear them secondhand. Since the board met on a weekday morning, most working people could not attend meetings in person. I started recording meetings so that I could bring that communication to my constituents via my website, and one of the commissioners was very frustrated and asked our attorney if it was legal for a commissioner to record public meetings. I found the question to be odd, especially as s/he even stated the obvious—that it was supposedly a *public* meeting. After this interesting dialogue, I spoke with other elected officials over the next few years and found out that efforts to limit public discourse with citizens are somewhat common in various regions of our nation.

One commissioner from another Minnesota county (Freeborn) shared with me how county board members grabbed his recorder and smashed it on the floor as they thought it was wrong to record their public meetings. The Clark County Park Board, Illinois, refused to allow public input at a meeting, leading to an eventual citizens' arrest by two brave military veterans leveled against this corrupt board that had a backlog of financial improprieties that left this county in a financial mess.[18] When any government board puts up such strong barriers to communication with its constituents, we should be alarmed as it often means that there is information or behavior that they do not want us to know about.

The State of Minnesota was just given a D- grade in transparency to the public due to a range of reasons, including minimal documentation of per diem pay (only three states scored a C- or better according to the Center for Public Integrity).[19] In 2015 alone, Minnesota state legislators received about $2 million in per diems, which is essentially extra pay for legislators without income-tax liabilities. The most frustrating part of this expenditure is that there is minimal accountability for these funds. In the real business world, when an employee asks his or her employer for reimbursement for a legitimate business expense, he or she has to submit documented receipts as the employer needs these to verify the expense, plus the government, ironically, may require these documents at tax time as part of its auditing practices. It is very difficult to say that the government is being transparent with what it does with our tax dollars when it requires us to document our expenditures while it is not required to do the same.

Backroom deals are almost always both unfair and unproductive for the public good. I know one county that hired the second-best person for a key new position within the county. When I asked why the highest-rated candidate did not get the job, I was told that their board had made an informal agreement (illegally, I would add) that they would not hire any candidate until they could agree on a 5–0 vote as they did not want to offend the new person with any dissenting votes. It is dangerous to make votes under false pretenses. From my business viewpoint, I would have stood up and voted what I thought was best for the organization I represented, and if I were outvoted, I would have set up a personal meeting with the winning candidate to congratulate him or her on winning the job, voice my concerns in a professional manner, and start a dialogue of how to most effectively work together going forward. Unfortunately, that direct leadership style does not happen often enough with disingenuous politicians. When our elected officials are willing to make an admittedly wrong decision for political favors, it is easy to understand why Americans are so disenfranchised from their shattered politics.

At the federal level, the number of backroom deals between the two parties has gone so far that legitimate tasks are rarely undertaken without some form of give and take for future political favors. The amount of indebtedness internally among politicians brings the spotlight of the decision-making process away from the constituents they are entrusted to serve and puts it on self-serving interests that are made with personal future favors as the more important criteria. This is not the American political system that citizens want; it is corruption gone awry.

YELLING AND NAME-CALLING HAVE REPLACED HONEST DEBATE

Sustainability of a nation is a serious issue, and the maturity level for taking on these tough questions is too often lower than grade-school mentality.

Have you ever listened to a contentious discussion within your government? I find it amazing that we teach our children not to be bullies, yet our elected officials often govern this way as they prioritize power over service and strong-arming unacceptable policies over rational and defendable positions. I have had middle- and high-school-aged children observe political debate, and they often talk about the childish experience as reminding them of their kindergarten or first-grade school days. Perhaps our political elites could learn from our children how to debate in a civil manner.

There is a reason the topics of sex, religion, and politics are often deemed off limits in many family or social circles: they can be very emotional and divisive. It can be very easy to share opinions about controversial subjects and watch the tone of voice quickly spiral out of control. Unfortunately, these heated discussions often create such emotional intensities that cloud rational and reasoned discussions about the role of governance and politics in America today. Yes, many of us have opinions, but as we argue our points, too often we create barriers to real communication regarding the severity of these issues. Politicians are generally more adept at speaking than listening, and thus the voice of the masses, even when speaking loudly, is oftentimes not clearly heard as inherent biases cloud the decision-making processes that are already in place well before any level of public input may be allowed on a given issue.

Unfortunately, discussions on serious issues too quickly turn into shouting matches over different ideologies. Obviously, tough issues can be very complex, and there usually is no magical solution; however, whatever the question is, new ideas and perspectives can often help sharpen the best answer. However, those ideas are often squashed early on by arrogant politicians who either think they know better or have an obligation to serve a different cause within their political circles.

I especially find it appalling how politicians cover for each other, whereas other industries discipline or punish inexcusable actions. For example, when I confronted an elected official about a suspected abuse of funds, the person readily admitted to it and paid back the political organization, but s/he screamed at me, saying this information better not go public. In my military days, actions like this usually ended up in a court martial or dishonorable discharge. In business, employees like this end up fired. In politics, these types of immoral actions are often covered up with threats of retribution from political elites.

Americans face serious issues from our local levels of government to our federal level, and it is time we put aside the first-grade mentality of name-calling and sound bites that hinder rational thoughts. More effective solutions need to be debated rather than superficial Band-Aid solutions that end up working poorly and costing us, the taxpayers, more in the end.

SUMMARY
The following are some of the key points from this chapter:

* American citizens are tired of the never-ending blame game of politics, and it is costing our nation greatly.
* Some politicians defer public policy and budgets to their staff which is a very dangerous practice as there is then no medium between the supplier and consumer.
* Many, if not most, public decisions are made in private settings.
* Transparency has given way to tradeoffs and backroom deals.
* Honest debate has been replaced by grade-school-level yelling in many political circles.

> *"A government by secrecy benefits no one. It injures the people it seeks to serve; it damages its own integrity and operation. It breeds distrust, dampens the fervor of its citizens and mocks their loyalty."*

> SENATOR RUSSELL B. LONG

CHAPTER 6

Entrenched System Stifles Genuine Public Service

• • •

Is our current political system of career politicians working for you?

THE TRAGIC REALITY IS THAT Americans are no longer in charge of our government as it has been taken over by a deep-rooted group of political elites that are more interested in power than public service. This reality is not just at the federal level; it is often even worse at many state and local levels of political office. The unfortunate result is that we have a system that is more interested in power and control than setting us free to pursue the American dream of endless opportunities for all as well as overseeing the delivery of respectable public services that are appreciated by constituents.

America continues to disintegrate from within as too many politicians double down on broken ideas. The fundamental result is that we now have political elites who fight harder for self-serving motives than what is best for the future of their constituents. This situation is very black and white for me as I recall my twenty-three years of service with so many military members who were willing to give everything, including the ultimate sacrifice of their lives, for a country they believed in. In politics, that love of nation rarely reaches that level of sacrifice as it is more about how to get to the pinnacle where one can make big bucks and gain power within the political system.

The entrenched system begins with our voting. One of the challenges of voting is that we often vote based on personality or likability more than realistic or proven abilities to make a promise and have the skills and character to make it happen to the best of their abilities. What I found in public office was that virtually all elected officials have some form of biases or pet projects that they may reveal in private settings, but those views change when they put on their public faces in front of their constituents. The bottom line is that all politicians have, to at least some degree, a higher level of confidence than most voters as they attempt to sway voters that they are the right choice. Many slick politicians have fooled voters into thinking that they genuinely care and are one of us, but I found that the real faces of elected officials often came out when they were working away from the public eye.

Our shattered politics has also taken us far away from truly fixing any of the many very serious challenges facing our great nation, with the constant focus on political ideology and bickering instead of pragmatic problem solving that you are more likely to find in family or business settings. The American mind-set is so entrenched in the failures of our shattered politics that it is alarmingly frightening or unreal when any politician attempts to offer up real solutions to our ever-growing problems. The result is far too many politicians that offer us weak, ineffective, and disingenuous leadership that works harder to appease voters than it does to identify commonsense solutions or free us to solve our own problems without excessive government intrusion.

In today's fast-pace world, citizens typically vote for candidates who are perceived as caring the most about their specific issues of concern, yet there is too little assessment given to how good things can be accomplished without continuing to punish taxpayers with more taxes. Public governance is *not* about good intentions; it is fundamentally about managing limited resources to resolve public issues. Think about it like this: we may care more about poor Uncle Bob, who struggles with paying off his credit cards, than Uncle Bill, who pays his bills but is not as friendly, but who would we choose to manage our own assets? With most Americans paying anywhere from one quarter to one half or more of their incomes to taxes, wouldn't it make more sense to vote for candidates whom we respect enough to manage our money and who most align with our values?

Adversity can be good for any organization as it can help bring urgency to fixing problems in a more effective manner. If America could only capture the negative energy it has toward its shattered politics and bring it forward in a manner that can create new options, citizens would gravitate toward problem-solving ideas more than a shattered political system that serves only a select few while the rest of us suffer the consequences of a weakened nation. One of the problems for American voters today is where to start slowing down government bureaucracy as it runs so deep in our system. For example, with almost seven thousand separate local governmental bodies in place, more than in any other state, it is difficult for voters in Illinois to truly analyze their voting options. This excessive number of layers of government makes it difficult as citizens don't know where to start identifying their local government.

A core responsibility of any elected official is to exhibit leadership in setting goals and a vision for its jurisdiction. Yet this is all too rare in politics as very few governmental organizations have goals, plans, visions, or any strategy for improving themselves and the services they provide to the public. Talk is cheap, but effective management of public resources is hard work, and we too often let politicians get away with the lazy answer of politics via the status quo. Accountability and measuring progress or returns on investments are rare concepts in the political world. Instead, it has become an ever-evolving set of new ideas about more and more. No wonder government has grown out of control. There is minimal definition of what it does and, perhaps more importantly, what it does not do. Isn't this approach antiquated in modern-day America?

Citizens should be wary when politicians (policymakers) overtly work with staff outside of normal business. Separating policymakers from budget managers and staff is not easy to do, but it provides a cushion and trust level with the constituents who inherently believe there are built-in biases between these two parties. One dangerous breech of this is when politicians help staff; especially staffs that must go through the election process like some local levels of government do with offices such as auditor, attorney, and sheriff. We had one incident nearby where a group of concerned citizens watched a county commissioner put up lawn signs for one of these elected quasi-staff positions. This is dangerous, highly immoral, and certainly a conflict of interest since an elected official who is technically supposed to be the boss of an employee was seen working to expand his or her internal political network. This incident illustrates just how far some politicians will go to place their personal interests over the public interest. Following is an illustration of how elected officials must balance these competing interests. In general, when elected officials give more weight to internal political alliances than their taxpayers, public trust decreases.

Public Trust versus the Political System

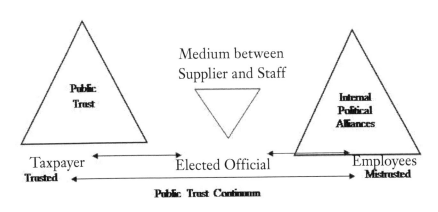

Much of our current political system uses antiquated ways of viewing assets. For example, in the public sector, employees are often classified as "permanent," while in the private sector, employees are typically referred to as "at will." These terms help illustrate the old ways of viewing employees as lifelong fixtures instead of assets who need to perform to maintain their at-will value within the organization. I know many great public-sector workers, but shouldn't they have to perform to similar standards and definitions as those working in the private sector? This different standard of public employee and private employee can also cause unnecessary hardship between service providers (public staff) and recipients (private-sector workers/taxpayers).

Just like in the business world, minimal contingency planning can hinder sustainability and efficiency and may be costly. For example, local governmental aid hand-downs are one of the top revenue sources for many local levels of government and are often used to create programs that appear to shift the funding burden away from the user. But in the end, we all pay for this redistribution of funds that goes through several bureaucratic agencies until it ends up becoming another unsustainable form of public service. The problem is that accountability for the public good is virtually impossible to evaluate as programs have become so intertwined with different funding sources. There are also so many hidden taxes and hidden levels of government, and without spending significant time and energy researching various public programs, it is very difficult for the average person to fully understand how costly various public programs are in our society.

Pure governance has given way to biases and personal agendas that are more selfish than service-oriented. Why do Americans so distrust and disrespect politicians? The primary reason is because politicians have exhibited more selfish actions in contrast to most other professions. Selfish motives far too often guide public policymaking at all levels of government and tarnish the value of public good.

This book is focused on the elected official who governs resources, including financial and human. From my view, there are many quality workers working within government to help serve the public. Unfortunately, the self-serving style of many politicians is demoralizing many great workers within the public sector. It is very difficult for workers to complain about mismanaged politicians as they obviously want to keep their jobs, but, believe me, if given a chance, many courageous workers would candidly admit how frustrating it is to work with politicians who think they know more than they truly do. The arrogance, combined with ignorance, of our politicians is not only hurting the citizens of our great nation, but it is also creating low morale within the public workplace for far too many. These hard workers know they have their hands tied unless the political system improves and respectability is brought back into office.[a]

The following are some of the key points from this chapter:

* Americans tend to vote more for likability than for pragmatic problem solvers as we are very skeptical of the long history of empty political promises.
* In general, politicians have big egos, and some are better at hiding their self-serving interests than others.
* Public value is in serious danger when elected officials campaign on behalf of elected staff candidates; this is a serious conflict of interest.
* The public is frustrated with public workers being treated as permanent assets, while the private sector deals with the realities of at-will employment.
* The ability of public employees to provide quality public services is negatively impacted when politicians mismanage this resource.

---

a I want to thank the many courageous staff members of local, state, and federal offices who provided me with insights over the past eight years into how our shattered politics creates significant challenges in the quality of delivering their services to their citizens.

*"The difference between a politician and a statesman
is that a politician thinks about the next election while
the statesman thinks about the next generation."*

James Freeman Clarke

CHAPTER 7

Has America Lost Its Culture of Self-Reliance?

• • •

"I predict future happiness for Americans if they can
prevent the government from wasting the labors of the
people under the pretense of taking care of them."

THOMAS JEFFERSON

IT IS IRONIC THAT OUR culture values choice so much, yet we willingly give away many of our choices and freedoms to a government that we do not respect. In addition, the number of examples of oppressive governments taking away individual freedoms is large and consistent throughout human history. When we ask government to take from others to give to those defined as needier, we give more power to our government. At some point, we will all eventually lose freedoms and privileges that a free society enjoys. Free stuff from the government is actually an oxymoron because for government to give something for free, it must first force taxation on someone else. During the roller-coaster ride of political paybacks, very few citizens will end up victorious except a small class of political elites and America will lose its identity as a self-sufficient nation that embodies freedom and the fair opportunity for all to prosper.

With a nation as diverse as America, it is very difficult to establish an optimal government that fits a wide range of values embodied in American citizenship. The original intent of America was to establish a limited government that provides its citizens with unlimited opportunities to succeed or fail within a free society of liberty and freedom for all. As the decades go by, cultures change, and so do the political priorities that go with that change. We have seen a seismic change in opinions over what America is about, but the one common denominator for a majority of Americans is that the current political arena does not reflect many of our core values.

In order to help identify the culture of America, I believe it is best to analyze it from an international perspective. What do Americans value that may be different from, or even the same as, other countries? One of the more interesting studies I found on this subject was "America's Thirteen Core Values," published in 1984 by L. Robert Kohls, executive director for the Washington International Center.[20] Based on his findings from over 30 years ago, Americans have thirteen core values:

America's Thirteen Core Values, By Dr. L. Robert Kohls

- Personal control over the environment
- Change
- Time and its control
- Equality/egalitarianism
- Individualism and privacy
- Self-help
- Competition and free enterprise
- Future orientation
- Action/work orientation
- Informality
- Directness, openness, and honesty
- Practicality and efficiency
- Materialism/acquisitiveness

Have these values changed much since 1984? I have reviewed these definitions of cultural values with hundreds of citizens between 2012 and 2016, and the answers I got were that this was a fairly strong starting point, with these modifications to the original thirteen values:

- Time and its control: the value of delayed gratification has eroded significantly in recent years
- Equality/egalitarianism: this has been modified by a strong push for greater class warfare
- Self-help: a growing belief that government is a self-help system
- Competition and free enterprise: this value has moderately decreased in recent years with more emphasis on entitlements and redistribution instead of self-reliance and free competition
- Future orientation: people are more skeptical of America having a better future

In addition to these four modifications, two additional values were very common among those interviewed:

- Citizens wanting more freedom to pursue their religion as they see fit without governmental judgment or restrictions outside of public safety
- Citizens embracing the value of technology to help communicate with each other and be more productive with their time

Americans value freedom to pursue religion as they see fit without governmental judgment or limitations. Our citizenship is getting tired of self-righteous and hypocritical politicians who act like they are better than everyone else. I am reminded of an incident that took place at a public political event when a politician told my wife that s/he did not believe I was a Christian, ironically in front of my pastor. The moral of this story is not about my faith but how political elites truly believe they are entitled to judge others in dangerous ways that are insulting to constituents. Most people I know, including myself, believe that God is the judge of our actions on earth, not politicians. It is a very dangerous slope when some politicians are so blatant in becoming moral judges as they generally are not a group that most of us respect. Perhaps that is a better role for individuals to fill with their clergy and their God?

Americans' growing dependence on technology is easy to see all around us with cell phones, iPads, and other technological tools being used by most adults and a growing number of children. Americans obviously value this tool to help them stay connected to personal, family, business, and other important matters.

With these modifications to Robert Kohl's original thirteen core values in place, we now have a revised current standard of fifteen cultural values that, in its simplified version, includes:

* Personal control over the environment (looking out for one's own self-interests)
* Change (progress via hard work and individual responsibility)
* Time and control (live-for-today mentality)
* Equality/egalitarianism (transition point between old-school values of everyone being created equal versus new-school views that emphasize economic class differences)
* Individualism and privacy (privacy and individuality are highly valued in the United States)
* Self-help (transition point between individual responsibility and the belief that government is there to help us)
* Competition and free enterprise (a majority of people support free competition, but there is a small, growing group that prefers socialistic redistribution)
* Future orientation (this value has essentially vanished but is wanted by many as it provides hope for future generations in our nation)
* Action/work orientation (we are very busy people)
* Informality (we are highly informal regarding authority and structure)

- Directness, openness, and honesty (bold and direct communication style)
- Practicality and efficiency
- Materialism/acquisitiveness (ability to obtain and protect material assets)
- Religious freedom (ability to pursue faiths that do not harm others without government restrictions)
- Technology (a valued tool for communications and productivity)

We are at a time when many of these values are still important to many Americans; however, they are being challenged by a group of political elites and special-interest groups that want to chip away at them. Our foundational principle of freedom is at stake as we identify the values that Americans want for a nation that is on the brink of collapse, but it has the historical fortitude to overcome serious challenges like our currently shattered politics.

Are these values still relevant today? I believe that politics, to a very large degree, often represent the exact opposite of many of these values. For example, let's review five of them:

- Competition and free enterprise versus political focus on abuse and control
- Future orientation versus blaming others for past problems
- Directness, openness, and honesty versus the opposite communication style of most politicians, which involves cunning and evasiveness
- Practical and efficient versus utopian promises and experimental ideas
- Acquiring materials respectfully through work versus taking an ever-increasing amount of materials through force

When the United States was founded in 1776 with an emphasis on self-reliance, it was structured in a manner illustrated in figure 1, the original governance structure of America. In this illustration, citizens were the primary stakeholders in the eighteenth century, responsible for ensuring freedom and opportunity for all to pursue their dreams in this new nation. Citizens held the responsibility of preserving the United States. Next in line for authority and respectability were businesses, both big and small. Charities and the church were placed fairly high in the hierarchy of things in which individuals could participate as they freely chose to do or not to do. The media, primarily local newspapers, was a moderately important mechanism for communicating the affairs of government to the people in a straightforward manner. Lobbyists or special-interest groups were essentially unheard of back then as citizens were united in their desires to protect their liberties and work together toward building a sustainable nation that was different than where they came from. Finally, at the bottom of the hierarchy was government, with its respected elected officials who often made great sacrifices in family or work to temporarily help their government develop policies at the local level.

Figure 1
Original Governance Structure of America

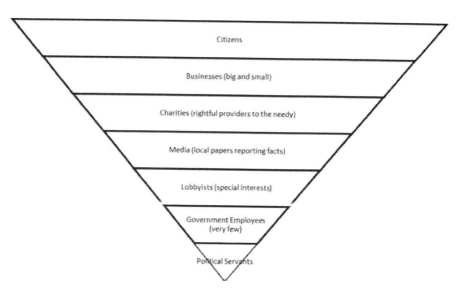

Over the course of many years, the top-heavy emphasis of citizen-led governance intended by the founding fathers of America has reversed as our nation gradually kept giving away its responsibilities to its elected officials and a growing network of supportive political operatives within the system. As figure 2 shows, the role of government has gone from the bottom of the pyramid to the top. Not only has government reversed its role in American prioritization, it has added numerous layers of government. A government intended to be focused on the local level grew out of proportion to an out-of-control federal government. In addition to the federal level, the expansion of state and local government brings our dependence on government to even higher, unsustainable levels.

Beyond the direct governing organizations represented by our elected officials, several notable influencing peripheral groups have increased in power and authority within America. Special-interest groups and lobbyists have combined efforts to coerce government to forcefully take more from the producers and give to their chosen special-interest groups. The media is still a player in the dissemination of public affairs but has now switched from reporting news to entertaining us with news that includes numerous special-interest efforts that are often out of balance with the heartland news of American prosperity generated by hardworking citizens and successful businesses. In addition, facts are often spiced up with opinions to further entertain us. Near the bottom of the food chain in America's shattered politics is business, now divided into small and large designations that struggle to keep up with ever-evolving regulations. Finally, the smallest voice of today's modern political system is the taxpayer, who foots much of the bill for this shattered politics.

The numbers of people and hours devoted to preserving our shattered politics is mindboggling. And the political elite will obviously not give up their power because they are the primary beneficiaries of this system. America needs to bring back some resemblance of the first pyramid if we are going to stop from going under in debt and crumbling from within our own broken country.

Figure 2
Revised Governance Structure of America in 2016

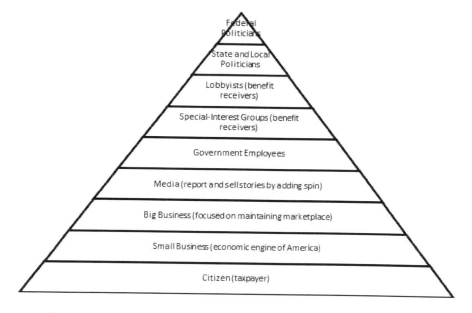

There is a rapidly increasing number of Americans who feel displaced and that their country is being taken away from them. This growing disconnect between the political system and the real world is a major concern. Americans want political choices that align more with our values.

Some of the key points from this chapter include:

* America has a very diverse culture, and setting up an ideal political system to meet these unique values is a daunting challenge.
* The hierarchy of America's political system and its citizens has reversed itself from the original intent with politicians moving from the bottom of the pyramid to the top, while citizens have moved from the top to the bottom.
* The political values in America are often vastly different than our mainstream cultural values.

- America's cultural values have changed over the past several decades, but the predominant culture of mainstream America is still based on a high interest in freedom to make our families' lives better as we see fit.
- Further movement away from citizenship to a system of political elitism will result and has resulted in America's lost identity as a nation of self-reliant individuals based on free competition to becoming a nation that is more controlled by government than self.

"Our lives begin to end the day we become
silent about things that matter."

MARTIN LUTHER KING JR.

CHAPTER 8

Earning Money versus Easy Money versus Taking Money

• • •

"Opportunity is missed by most people because it is dressed in overalls and looks like work."

THOMAS EDISON

THE OLD ADAGE OF FOLLOWING the money is especially true in politics. We have the privilege of living in a nation that provides all of us the opportunity and freedom to pursue our dreams however we want to define them, including the free choice to work for someone else, go to college and learn a profession, or start one's own business. Just as Zig Ziglar once said, he chose to weigh XYZ pounds because no one ever forced him to eat or exercise. Americans have the same right, within their own abilities and efforts, to pursue a wide range of social and economic paths for themselves and their families. Perhaps it is time to stop making excuses for the economic plights that arguably are there, as well as the weight problems. Since we still have the freedom to choose our paths, perhaps we should focus on the endless possibilities that once made America the leading nation in so many ways.

Throughout the years that included entry-level jobs early in my life, six years of college, a professional marketing career of twenty years, a military career of twenty-three years (some part time in the reserves and some full time during deployments), and political service of six years, I have seen a range of ways to earn and manage money as viewed through different spectrums, including family, business, military, and political. Viewed through a political spectrum, receipt of money boils down to these three actions:

- Earning money, which is the fundamental backbone of America, where citizens have the freedom to work hard for the right to compensation and benefits
- Easy money, which stays within the political system
- Taking money, which has been elevated in political circles as a fair means for taking from someone who earned it, skimming some off the top for the political system, and then "generously" giving to someone who did not earn it and could become a pawn of the political system

EARNING MONEY

As I review more of the history of the founding fathers who designed America, I appreciate the sacrifice and fortitude so many had in establishing principles that would separate us from our British roots and guide us in how governance would better serve the constituents. Similar to that in today's American military culture, there was a great respect for the courage and sacrifices made by leaders to take a bold stance in bringing America to greatness. A common theme was that most public servants back in that day did their public service because of an unyielding love for the start of a new country, the United States. Those were the days when public service was generally undertaken with respected principles and limits that fostered liberty and justice equally for all in a fairly pure manner. Today's political principles represent a much different view.

When discussing the various careers where someone can earn money for hard work, I like to start with our military, police officers, and

firefighters since these professions are highly respected and generally underpaid, and these workers are typically willing to give everything, including their lives and time with their families, for the protection of others and
the flag that our freedoms represent. There are many other honorable jobs
or professions that result in the creation or delivery of productive goods
and services that can be enjoyed by others within a free nation.

In general, people make money through hard work, sweat equity, risk, education, and applying themselves within the marketplace.
Fundamentally, I believe that hardworking entrepreneurs and workers are
the engine that makes this country run. I also believe that it can be very
dangerous to make generic statements that the rich are evil as that leads
to stereotyping in a derogatory manner in many ways that are often not
true and undermine the value of people working hard to make it in our
great nation.

As a nation that prides itself on self-reliance, America will be much
better off going forward if we recognize that earning money is a very personal choice, and it can be dangerous in a free society to demoralize those
who make good money. For example, I know many who complain about
how much talented athletes and actors make; I wonder why anyone would
complain as people are freely willing to give them money for what they
do well. Unfortunately, we live in an upside-down world where politicians
criticize the rich while they pocket our money and become rich off the
work of others.

Easy Money

I will never forget that one of my first phone calls after winning the election to the county board was from an elected official, and it went like this:
"Congratulations on winning your election. I just want you to know that
if you ever can't make it to any meeting, just let me know so I can attend as
I can use the extra per diem money."

I found this call to be disturbing and so odd after serving twenty-three years in the military, where I was so used to hearing significantly different reasons for soldiers entering this form of public service and taking on extra duties. Beyond the blunt answer, I found it strange that the primary intent of going to additional meetings was not to hear about how our county should work with the particular organization but rather how this person could personally benefit from attending. I later found out that in addition to our base pay of approximately twenty-six thousand dollars, there was a whole lot of additional financial rewards of being an elected official that the average citizen does not realize. For example, we had several commissioners who made more than double their base salary with all the fringe benefits added to their cost to the taxpayers (nice pay for a part-time job).

As I served the residents of Isanti County as a county commissioner, I reflected on the challenges associated with this elected office in contrast with my public service in the US military. When comparing the responsibilities and rewards of both positions, I found it alarming that our local taxes paid me about three to five times as much to serve as an elected official as I was paid to serve as a major in the US Army Reserves, even though the responsibilities I had in the military were much bigger (figure 3). It made me realize the hypocrisy of how many politicians felt they were underpaid for what they did, whereas I rarely heard military soldiers complain about their pay. The primary difference seemed to be that soldiers generally love their country and the honor they had in helping protect the nation they loved, while many politicians viewed elected office as a place of entitlement to earn extra money or meet their egotistical needs.

Political pay is public record; however, too many politicians have found creative ways to make more income from their public service, both from the taxpayers and elsewhere. A few examples include:

* Per diems, nontaxable income

- Healthcare and other benefits for part-time work not normally included in other part-time jobs
- Service on other related or charitable boards
- Post-public-service career in lobbying

Responsibilities and Pay Comparison:
Military versus Politician
Figure 3

Responsibility	US Army Reserves Major $10–15K per year	Isanti County Commissioner $30–50K per year*
Time Commitments	2–4 full days each month, 2 weeks full time each year, and numerous other meetings	2–4 half-day core meetings each month and numerous other meetings
Personnel Management	BN commander typically responsible for 500 plus soldiers	Manage a staff of approx. 220 full- and part-time employees
Resource Management	Average responsibility for a field-grade officer is $100 million or more in property and equipment management	Manage an annual budget of approx. $34 million
Sacrifices	Willing to sacrifice life and time away from family	Willing to be a public servant for constituents

*Including base pay, per diems, and health insurance

At the federal level, US Congress members have the fundamental job of establishing a budget and yet fail to do so virtually every year, but they have no problem giving themselves hefty raises and additional perks each year. It makes one wonder if the genuine interest of our political elites is in serving others or making easy money.

Taking Money

> *"A businessman cannot force you to buy his product; if he makes a mistake, he suffers the consequences; if he fails, he takes the loss. A bureaucrat forces you to obey his decisions, whether you agree with him or not...If he makes a mistake, you suffer the consequences; if he fails, he passes the loss on to you, in the form of heavier taxes."*

> Ayn Rand

The Declaration of Independence begins with the premise of moral equality—that all are created equal as defined by our natural rights to life, liberty, and the pursuit of happiness. We do not get these rights from government; on the contrary, whichever rights or powers that government has come from us. Who is the boss? We, the people! The purpose of government is not to create these rights and obligations but simply to recognize and enforce them.[21] This principle has vanished in America today as politicians are dictating what to do with over 40 percent of the financial assets of our nation.

Though America was built on many exceptional principles, the founding fathers also knew that special efforts would be needed to preserve the freedoms and liberty of a great nation. As James Madison once said, "Liberty finds few friends amongst political insiders," and "Power is not alluring to pure minds." Unfortunately, because of a political system that encourages "free" handouts without the sweat equity that once made us a great nation, America is quickly losing many of its high standards within the world economy. We do not prosper as a nation when we reward unproductivity as defined within the worldwide marketplace.

The political will of America has been overtaken by special interests and corruption, which detracts from moral reasoning and fairness within our shattered politics. The result is that a nation built on self-reliance has given in to expecting bailouts from others, and our elected officials then undertake the act of forcefully taking other people's money without restraint. In the past, the American culture looked on other options outside of government to help take care of us, whether family, church, or neighbors. The job of far too many politicians has unfortunately devolved into showing that they "care" about fixing various social problems, and they can only fix them with other people's money. Redistribution to the poor is not only not helping, but it has done much to ruin the dignity and souls of the individuals who can make it further on their own or with the help of those who genuinely care about their well-being. This may sound overly direct, but government simply cannot be your friend to help you in a long-term, sustainable, and liberating manner. Concerned citizens need to look at the many failed entitlement programs and realize that tough love is almost always more effective in improving the long-term well-being and spirit of the human being than entitlements.

Public charity is forced charity and is not a virtue but a vice. It has had many damaging effects on our culture as it replaces great nonprofit charities that are operated by those close to the situation who are vested stakeholders in providing first-class service while respecting basic return-on-investment principles. Money speaks loudly in America as a generally free nation; we invest our hard-earned financial resources in those items we need or want. This goes both ways: funding is also a negative when spent on misguided causes or efforts. Look at our investments:

* Most people buy goods or services that they value and are willing to pay for.
* Most people donate to their favorite charities because they willingly support the cause of the organizations.

* "Free" handouts by politicians are usually more about control than about genuine help.
* Taxes are forced payments with many questionable returns on investment.

We have come to a time in America when people believe that it is a right for politicians to forcefully confiscate tax dollars from the rich so that the poor can benefit. In a truly free nation, this fundamentally goes against the concept of willfully helping those in need.

Whatever happened to the American pride in working hard to earn the items you need or even want?

SUMMARY
Some of the key points from this chapter are as follow:

* An overwhelming majority of Americans work hard for their money, and shaming them for their success does not help our nation, which used to value success.
* There are many ways to make easy money in today's shattered politics, and the political elites do not want us to know that.
* America's foundation of individual self-reliance is being taken away by political elites who now force taxation at 40 percent of our GDP.
* Forcefully taking money from others for charitable redistribution is not a virtue but a vice.

"What is your fair share of what somebody else has earned?"

THOMAS SOWELL

CHAPTER 9

Nice Guys Finish Last

• • •

*We teach our children not to be bullies, yet far too many politicians
govern this way as they prioritize power and control over service.*

I BELIEVE THAT MOST AMERICANS are at least somewhat nice, compassionate, friendly, and agreeable to helping others in need. In general, these
are admirable qualities that can benefit society greatly. However, these
qualities can also be taken advantage of by power-hungry groups like political elites who often prey on quiet citizens to gain more power over our
lives. According to Wiktionary, the definition of "nice guys finish last"
is "People who are decent, friendly and agreeable tend to be unsuccessful
because they are outmaneuvered or overwhelmed by others who are not so
decent, friendly or agreeable."

Nice guys are finishing last in America's shattered politics. Tensions
are high, and blame is everywhere, as America self-destructs due to a political elite class that has taken over our country and is fighting hard to
preserve their power and control but failing to make America any better. Lost in this lust for power is the importance of service, respecting
hardworking taxpayers, and even caring about the opinions or concerns
expressed by a dissatisfied citizenship. Arrogant politicians think they
know what is better for us than we do. In sum, the political elites are
fighting a lot harder than the hardworking taxpayers, and the nice guys, or

producers, are finishing last in the battle to regain a self-reliant America that prospered for over two hundred years.

Using the definition by Wiktionary for "nice guys finish last," let's review how abusive politicians are defeating the citizens. First, many politicians are extremely skilled at outmaneuvering their constituents. Outmaneuvering refers to using skills and cunning to secure an advantage over someone, not to help serve them. Politicians have become very adept at defeating or frustrating citizens as they claim to have all the answers, and we become subservient to their decisions, frustrating a once-vibrant nation as we literally lose our freedom and liberty to a growing beast that controls more of our lives.

Politicians are also often exceptional at pulling on the heartstrings of its citizens with ideas that demonstrate care and compassion with minimal connection to reality or with respect to the true costs of these ideas. During these heated arguments, the concept of public service is forgotten far too often. Many of the political elite are very skilled at saying, "You just don't understand," to their constituents. If we don't understand something, it would be nice if politicians would respectfully articulate what it is we are missing as they are supposedly there to serve us, aren't they?

Today's shattered politics is often formed by an inner circle of the political elite. For example, the primary goal at most caucus levels is how to best protect their party's power rather than how to better serve the public. Even caucus votes are somewhat meaningless as raw vote totals count less than those of super delegates. Presidential races are shaped more than a year out by a media that provides us with poll after poll after poll to help "inform us" how other voters are thinking. Following the political dialogue of our nation is a tiring job that exhausts most of our hardworking citizens.

Another tactic used frequently by the political elite is overwhelming us with information and phases to understand their system. In fact, many of their policies are so overwhelming that the politicians don't even have time to read what they are voting on, as we are reminded with our recent healthcare legislation, which passed with some of Congress admitting that they never even read the language of the bill. If they are not reading their policies that they are enacting on us, how are busy Americans supposed to keep up with the ever-increasing legislation that is smothering our nation in red tape?

Has anyone noticed just how nice politicians can be during campaign season but how they become different people once in office? Unfortunately, politics has become a contact sport in America, where many good-hearted people who want to make their community a better place are left to watch things crumble around them as louder voices take charge, resulting in less freedom for us citizens. The quiet voice of the majority is being squashed by special interests, vested stakeholders, and political insiders who have gained power and do not want to give it up unless we, the people, force the system to revert back to genuine public service as a priority. Politics truly is an ugly, full-contact sport as those within the bully pulpit will fight hard to keep their power, and the quiet citizens of our nation get pushed aside.

The voice of the average taxpaying citizen is very small compared to the internal voices that help shape the decisions of politicians. There is a built-in bias that favors the consumer of tax funds more than the supplier of the taxes. Some examples include:

* Public employees: Especially at the local level of government, politicians work closely with the employees who undertake the work of the governing agency. Their needs, as well as wants, are expressed on an ongoing, frequent basis.
* Lobbyists: Just walk the halls of Congress in DC or your state capital someday, and you will see full-time lobbyists there virtually nonstop. Their purpose is to persuade politicians to give more

to their special-interest needs while trying to justify or hide the true costs to be borne by taxpayers.

* Fellow politicians: On most governing boards, important decisions cannot be made without a majority vote. Thus, backroom deals and tradeoffs happen nonstop. When politicians find other co-conspirators who care more about getting power off each other than the constituents they serve, the taxpayer pays for this self-serving approach to governance.
* Other advocates, who are all in line asking for their handouts.
* Politicians who know how to work the system far too often get rewarded with reelection and the ongoing mess gets worse.

I can respect politicians who fight for their constituents, even if I disagree with their conclusions. However, far too much political disagreement takes place over how to best protect the existing system rather than how to best represent the citizens. For example, redistricting occurs every ten years in America, which can be a good thing for organizing political voting interests in some form of logical manner. However, redistricting decisions are mostly based on personal biases and political pitting rather than what's best for the constituents. In other words, voters are grouped based on what is best for the politicians and how they can best keep power, *not* the logical groups that might make more sense from the citizens' perspective. For example, redistricting in Illinois has historically been slanted so much and its voting blocs so entrenched that there is often minimal new competition for political seats.

Lies and distortions do not help anyone or improve the public service of government. We all know of lies, deception, and unbelievable statements made by politicians to help persuade voters one way or the other. It is amazing how far people will go to distort reality. I remember my second month in county office when there was a harsh letter to the editor about my "disrespectful tone of voice" regarding a disagreement I had about a proposed new comprehensive plan. I remember calling the person who wrote the opinion piece and asking where he was sitting in the audience that he perceived my tone as being disrespectful; he quickly admitted that he was not even at the meeting. I found out that this person was the campaign manager for one of the other commissioners, and this response was submitted even though there was no validity to the point being made. It was because of these made-up stories that I decided to record our meetings so the public could hear for themselves and judge the intent and tone of public dialogue for themselves. Working with political elites, this was my first awakening that bringing the political conversation closer to the public was not wanted, as their resistance revealed.

The heavyweight champions of political debate include the politicians themselves, lobbyists who have made major impacts, and other special-interest groups. Their voices have been loud and have slanted discussions toward more involvement from government to establish new levels of rights and power of government and less liberty for the individual. They have fought an impressive fight, and the loser has been the general American population, which has idly sat on the sidelines, grumbling about their ever-increasing taxes and the continued takeovers of their liberties. In the ongoing battle of politics, nice guys are truly finishing last. But this is an ongoing battle, and the time for the nice guys to stand up and have their voices be heard is rapidly coming upon us as the revolt against our shattered politics is reaching a crescendo of ugliness that has concerned citizens ready to speak up.

Some of the key points from this chapter include the following:

* Americans are generally decent, friendly, and agreeable, and the political elite have taken advantage of their good natures.
* Working-class America is taking a knockout punch as political elites fight hard to protect their system and personal privileges.
* Many politicians are very skilled at attacking people and not addressing issues.

* Many politicians fight harder to protect their self-interests and entitlements than they do to serve their constituents.
* The politicians are winning the fight to control America, but they are fighting a foundational soul of America that is preparing to take on the political elites and regain our country as the land of the free and home of the brave.

"In the end, people will remember not the words of our enemies, but the silence of our friends."

MARTIN LUTHER KING JR.

PART 2

Practical Steps Concerned Citizens Can Take to Regain Our Lost Government

CHAPTER 10

Winning Our Country Back

• • •

*It's time for the citizens of the United States to take back a political
system that has lost touch with the intended role of public service.*

AMERICA HAS A BIG MESS on its hands, and fixing it will not be easy.
However, I strongly believe in the American spirit and that we can overcome the challenges associated with corrupt, self-serving, and dysfunctional politicians as Americans have overcome many other adversities
over our past 240 years. One example that gives me hope for the future is
the high standard set by a parallel service organization, our US military.
Military and political organizations are quite similar as they both manage
tax-generated resources to accomplish a mission related to security and
safety. Both jobs have a narrowly defined mission with complexities that
can make the responsibilities expand without establishing some boundaries. A fundamental difference is that one organization is significantly
appreciated by the masses of Americans, while the other is generally not
respected as an effective organization.

Looking back in history to the late 1960s and early '70s, it was a tur-
bulent time in American culture, and the military was far too often poorly
viewed by a large segment of the population as soldiers returning from
Vietnam were often spat on and ridiculed in public places. Fast forward to
America's view of our military post-9/11, and the general public sentiment

is now much better, including standing ovations and special levels of recognition for service members at many public events. America's respect for the military veteran has gone from miserable to highly respected in just over forty years. We need a turnaround like that in American politics, but what are the steps we need to take to start our transition back to the great nation of America? Let's review some of the key improvements undertaken during the last four-plus decades by the US military that may be relevant to making necessary improvements in our shattered politics. Please note that this commentary is made with full respect for our military service members throughout the history of the United States.

- Today's military purpose is a more personalized mission as current service members generally have a stronger commitment to the US cause of fighting back against terrorism than the vaguer, more external purpose of the war in Vietnam.
- The pain of terrorism was brought closer to home, on US soil rather than overseas, so public appreciation for taking on the enemy is stronger.
- Volunteerism for military service peaked, and recruiters were able to bring in great recruits with an increased pool of candidates as opposed to forced drafting during the Vietnam era.
- The population is better able to see the positive results of victory more clearly through mass communications in today's smaller world.

Over the past several years, I have had the honor of working with several thousand military veterans in various capacities. The pride of these current soldiers and veterans was evident in many of these conversations, as well as their growing concern for the eroding freedoms in our nation. During these conversations, their first concern was almost always the families of soldiers separated for military duties; next was usually concerns over our shattered politics. As I reviewed the problems associated with self-serving politicians with my network of military veterans, specific attributes kept coming up as major differences between military leadership and what they were observing in the political arena. These qualities, which were identified during conversations with thousands of military veterans over the past four years, are shown in table 1.

Table 1
Differences between Political and Military Leadership*

Issue	Political	Military
Leadership style	Appease with empty promises	Deliver strong results
Rules of law and moral responsibility	Minimal belief that laws and rules apply to them	Strict moral and legal obligation to follow laws and rules
Commitment to service	Selfish service to oneself and the internal political system	Selfless service to others and a cause bigger than themselves
Honesty and integrity	Voter deception is very common	Being truthful, straightforward, and candid is required
Training	Minimal training for being a public servant	Extensive training on leadership, mission, and taking on adversities
Communication style	Evasive and politically correct style	Direct, empowering & purposeful
Principles versus personalities	Personalities influence decisions more than principles	Principles drive the mission; personalities are secondary
Conflict of interests	Interact with staff, and that voice is louder than constituents'	Officers separated from enlisted to minimize conflicts and risks

Motivation tactics	Persuade with fear	Build unit strength with courage
Respecting different backgrounds/views	Disrespectful toward op-posing views	Appreciate diversity in other service members
Problem solving	Make calculated decisions based on political gain	Make decisive deci-sions that are best for the mission
Accountability to stakeholders	Accountable more to political system and less to constituents	Accountable equally to military unit and nation they represent
Discipline	Instant gratification with few restraints	Delayed gratification with self-restraints
Standards	Rarely set higher stan-dards or goals to work toward	Set high standards and train vigorously to achieve results
Defined timeline of service	Endless decades of service available without term limits	Service time defined in number of years and/or retirement
Punctuality	Often late with no penalties	On time or harshly penalized
Organizational mission	An undefined mission that fosters out-of-control growth	A narrowly defined mis-sion shapes priorities and purpose
Primary purpose	Get elected, reelected, and grow the system	Defend nation against all enemies, foreign and domestic

*Table 1 represents a summary of concerns and differences expressed to me by several thousand military veterans, military family members, and concerned citizens during phone, in-person and e-mail conversations between 2012 and 2016. These views do not reflect any official position of the military or any specific political organization but rather are a collection of individual opinions expressed over a four-year period.

Since a very small percentage of Americans serve in the US military today, our general understanding of what makes it work so effectively is unclear to many. Most nonveterans respect the abilities of our military to overcome very dangerous situations but know very little about the training, sacrifice, and discipline that goes into making our military service members strong public servants and defenders of our nation. For the American shattered politics to be improved upon, we need citizens to understand the differences between political and military leadership and demand a higher level of genuine public service attributes going forward from our elected officials.

Fixing our shattered politics will require extensive leadership and commitment by many concerned citizens. We will need to train an army of concerned citizens on the foundation of America, identify the most fixable problems, and implement the necessary changes to bring politicians back on the right track of serving their constituents first. Whether we want to admit it or not, we as a society are highly dependent on government for many reasons. Even if this dependence is reduced, say, 10 to 25 percent, which would be a remarkable feat considering the greed for power currently in place within much of politics, we still need good governance to help America move forward as a strong nation in our ever-changing world.

At the heartbeat of America is a conscience that loves to be free and values choice. Deep down, a vast majority of individuals will generally want to make their own decisions and reap the rewards of their work. Words are cheap; we need decisive leadership that can effectively capture the heartbeat of mainstream America and bring those values back into our shattered politics before it's too late. The rights to freedom and liberty belong to the people, not the government, and the task is to bring genuine servant leaders to the political system who want to return power to the people, not themselves.

Before taking action to solve any problem, it is always wise to identify the problem and the best courses of action ahead of time. Concerned citizens can begin by identifying which political organizations (local, state, or federal) they believe have the largest problems. When it gets down to the political system, remember that systems at their core are people. However, we must also remember to not single out any one political person since most political organizations vote on a majority rule. Thus there may be one "problem child," but those problems cannot be manifested into poor legislation without other co-conspirators.

After determining which political organizations you believe are the most damaging, you can start honing in on the real problems. The earlier chapters of this book reveal some of the major hidden problems in politics, but you may uncover others as you take a closer look. Some of these major problems, as discussed previously, could include the following:

- Lack of transparency: Are meetings recorded for public review? Is citizen input welcomed at their meetings? Is there honest debate and discussions, or do most issues seem to be already settled before going public?
- Purpose: Does the governing board appear to care most about the citizens it governs, or other special interests, or other political members for political tradeoffs?
- Follow the money: Ask to see the budget, and ask questions. If there is reluctance to show you the public budget, it is high time to be suspicious.
- Vision and focus: Ask if the organization has any goals, codes of ethics, or principles that guide its mission.

Some may say that greed in America is with the "evil rich," but I would argue that greed and an out-of-control obsession with power is much worse with the general profession of politician than any other group at this time. So what can we do about it? I believe that the time is now for taking our country back and bringing back a political system that serves us without enslaving us with its abusive power and control.

Some of the key points from this chapter are as follow:

* America's political situation is a mess and fixing it will not be easy.
* One example of a similar public service organization that over- came a negative public perception and enhanced its status is the US military over the past 40 years.
* Most American's know very little about the details on how our military leaders achieve great accomplishments as our military veteran presence in America is quickly shrinking.
* There are vast differences between political and military leaders, and our shattered politics would improve greatly if we brought in more of the military leadership qualities into our governance.
* Military veterans fight for freedom and Americans also value this attribute, whereas that opinion does not resonate as strongly in political circles.

"You cannot escape the responsibility of tomorrow by evading it today."

ABRAHAM LINCOLN

CHAPTER 11

Taking Action

• • •

"If we do not change our direction, we will end up where we were going."

Ancient Chinese proverb

Based on conversations at local coffee shops, adult watering holes, and other social settings, I hear an overwhelming majority of concerned citizens griping about politicians. With elected officials making up one of the lowest-respected professions, it makes sense. The problem is that never-ending griping about a problem does not help the situation unless proactive steps are taken to correct it. Since it is doubtful that a majority of politicians are going to fix something they can't even agree is a problem or frankly do not want or need to change, it is also doubtful that many issues won't be fixed or even improved upon until the voting citizens of our country come together and demand improvements by our elected officials.

Complaining is a lazy way of addressing problems, while taking action to improve a negative situation involves time, energy, and often sacrifices to make significant political as well as cultural changes. As with our brave military, who sacrifice so much to protect our nation from our enemies, I believe the time is now for citizens to stand up against our greatest current threat to the freedoms enjoyed by Americans, namely a shattered political system that does not represent the best interests of a free nation. Unfortunately, we are at a time when many people complain about politicians and do nothing to very little to correct the problem, so it continues to worsen in front of our very eyes. Simply put, we need more concerned citizens getting involved to bring America's shattered politics back into the hands of the people who value freedom and liberty more than the status quo, where our political system abusively rules over its citizens.

Table 2 shows some examples of talking points for concerned citizens as they bring these conversations to their social networks as well as their elected officials.

Table 2
Talking Points for Concerned Citizens

Issue	Typical Political Speak	Rebuttal Talking Points
Fair share	Politicians say citizens need to pay their fair share for increases to their political system.	It is not fair for hardworking taxpayers to pay more for our political system than our housing.
Transparency	We are not able to share some information about *our* public expenditures and priorities.	Technically, it is *our* funds you are entrusted to spend with *our* oversight, and we are entitled to see *our* tax dollars at work.
Courage	We get requests from many organizations for many important priorities.	I can respect the demand on your position, and I would like to encourage you to be respectful of our limited resources as an overtaxed society as well.
I care for you and want your vote	What can I do to earn your trust and your vote?	I would like a government that promotes self-reliance more than more "free" handouts.

Political spin	I am a conservative.	Ask them to prove that they actually held taxes in check or reduced them (most cannot defend this).
Political spin, part 2	I am a liberal.	America currently spends almost half of our assets on taxes. What is your definition of how much more we should pay in a free society?
Evasive political speak	Political elites say, "You just don't understand."	You are right. Please explain why you support this and how it is a public good worth my tax dollars.
Campaign request for your vote	Political candidates ask for your vote.	Why are you running for office? How do you define public service? How do I know I can trust you?
Spending on more wants	XYZ is a need for our citizens.	Is it a need or a want, and is the goal to benefit the citizen or the politician?

Taking action will require a strong effort to overcome voter apathy as many citizens have given up and cannot vote for people or a system they do not respect. Though I can understand that, it will not solve the problem. One way to share the civic responsibilities that are so large in today's world is to establish small, nonpartisan groups of like-minded, concerned citizens to take turns observing your political organizations in action and discussing how improvements can be made. We need to communicate an expectation that elected officials: (1) work for us, (2) take their responsibility seriously and know that we are watching their actions, and (3) know that we expect integrity and fairness in how they make decisions that are for the betterment of the public and not payoffs to their power groups.

Citizens must be direct with their elected officials and be vigilant in demanding responses that follow the HOW principle:

* Honest: give us truth without deception
* Open: show us by their actions that they are open to hearing public concerns
* Willing to take a stand for their constituents without compromise for political payoffs

America's founding fathers designed our political system to be a citizen-led governance, which could work only if citizens were well informed and educated. If citizens were unable or unwilling to critically analyze public information, the nation could fall prey to slick politicians and unethical media coverage that presented biased information. The American political design was also based on citizens having the courage to stand by these principles that would keep us free from an abusive government. These principles were relatively easy to implement with a national population of one, ten, or even 25 million citizens, but when a population reaches over 300 million, like America has today, it becomes harder to hold tight to those original intentions of the constitution.

I believe that America's founding fathers had an intense desire to protect citizens from excessive government because they knew that politicians could not be trusted as they would eventually focus more on their own power and aspirations than on the intended purpose of public service. Fast forward to 2016, and public trust in our elected officials is extremely low as we recognize that many of their decisions help their internal stakeholders more than us everyday citizens. When we take action against any level of self-serving government, we must let the officials know that our trust in them is damaged when they enact legislation that benefits them more than the public they are elected to serve.

We must also remember that America is a constitutional republic. In a republic, your property is yours and is legally protected by the constitution. In a democracy, the majority rules, and if the majority decides they want your property, they could take it. In order to protect the rights of the individuals, it is imperative that we preserve the constitutional republic and not give power and authority to a dictatorship or big government as has been done by many other nations throughout human history. The design of a constitutional republic is an important tool for protecting hardworking Americans from abuses caused by public cries for class warfare, where some believe they are entitled to other people's property or assets.

Most citizens agree that we have a very serious problem with politicians in today's America, but what an honor it is to be part of the solution for fixing this big problem. Politicians know the easy road to power and dollars, while the citizens continue to suffer at the hand of those who know how to play the game. It is time for citizens to realize that their game of self-serving politics is destroying our nation, call them on it, and set up active measures to stop the downward spiral from this greatest threat to America in 2016. Table 3 shows a list of progressive steps that concerned citizens can take to help fix our shattered politics.

Table 3
Proactive Steps Concerned Citizens can take to
Fix Our Shattered Politics

1. Study political candidates and vote for those who best represent your values.
2. When meeting candidates, be sure to ask them why they are running for office.
3. Review budgets and minutes from your applicable local governmental offices.
4. Read the constitution, Declaration of Independence, and other important historical documents on the foundation of America.

5. Discuss the importance of America's foundational documents with your children and others within your spheres of influence.
6. Get informed on political issues via radio, television, and print materials.
7. Share respectful and insightful comments on political candidates through your local social media avenues.
8. Become a delegate at your caucus level, where political debate begins.
9. Volunteer to serve as a poll watcher or voting observer.
10. Establish a neighborhood group of citizens with similar concerns to take turns attending local or state political meetings and keeping each other informed.
11. Respectfully share your concerns, supported by facts whenever possible, with others over our shattered politics.
12. Write letters to your local newspaper editor that point out political problems or identify possible solutions outside of more government.
13. Ask your elected officials if they have and abide by a Code of Ethics and if they allow public input at their meetings.
14. Support candidates you believe in.
15. Consider running for office yourself or asking respected leaders to run.

Some of the key points from this chapter include the following:

* Virtually everyone complains about our shattered politics yet only a small percentage of these people take any proactive steps to improve the situation.
* If we do not change our downward spiral soon, we will greatly jeopardize the future of a once-mighty nation as we crumble from within.
* The Declaration of Independence is a powerful document that separates us from other political systems in many profound ways

and is a great document to reference as we identify what an improved political system looks like.

* Table 2 presents some rebuttal talking points for concerned citizens to use when communicating with their elected officials.

* A citizen-led government works only if our citizens are well informed and educated on effective public-service organizations, and this is becoming a greater challenge as our nation grows and is further separated from strong public-service principles.

> *"Getting off track is expectable, understandable and forgivable.*
> *Staying off track when you know you are off track is stupid."*

> LARRY WINGET

CHAPTER 12

Defining Legitimate Functions
of Our Government

• • •

"When the law of the land is used to limit government to its
legitimate functions of safeguarding persons and property,
people will be free to pursue their own happiness without
violating the rights of others, and justice will prevail."

JAMES MADISON

FUNDAMENTALLY, THE NUMBER-ONE JOB OF an elected official is to help ensure the safety of our citizens. From the commander-in-chief to congress,
and on to state and local offices, elected officials are responsible first for
ensuring safety for US citizens. Beyond safety, a strong infrastructure is
the cornerstone of a vibrant America, including reliable roads, shipping
ports, and airports to move people and supplies, safe water to treat and
move to consumers, and sufficient food supplies. Police and security personnel are very important and are the strong backbone to any safe society. Also protecting our borders from illegal immigration is important as
nearly every nation in the world has grasped this concept and established
immigration rules and protective measures that reflect the will of its people in a safe manner.

A reasonable expectation for a legitimate government includes the ability to spend within its means while defining means as limited, not limitless. Overspending and kicking the can downhill to future generations is not fair to them and can endanger our security with those to whom we are indebted to around the world. Perhaps the most significant actions that concerned citizens can ask of our government are to establish a goal and plan for reducing our $19-trillion national debt and to begin by reducing the overreach of the federal government to tax us and redistribute those collected funds back to the state and local levels of government. The political zeal for redistribution from federal to state and to local government is costing our nation dearly as higher levels of government tax us more, skim their administrative fees for handling these funds, and then redistribute the funds back to those who lobby the best for them.

It is very difficult for citizens in an overtaxed society like America to feel the benefit of their high taxes when they see nothing but out-of-control debt and a lost connection to the market realities of value, especially when someone from California pays federal taxes to Washington, DC, so he or she can pocket a few dollars and then ship some funds to somewhere else like Alaska to build a bridge. We need a better connection between taxation and representation, and the Tenth Amendment helps keep American taxes and programs local, but it has been twisted away from the original intention. The bottom line is that government works best at the local level as the closer the control of the government is to the people, the more interest and control citizens hold in political proceedings and operations, as well as understanding of the true needs and costs.

What should your government be doing? Each organization will answer this differently, though there are certainly many similarities between like organizations (such as rural towns, suburbs, metropolitan areas, states, and so forth). Unlike families and businesses, governments do not necessarily have to make good decisions to survive. With a power to tax to an uncontrollable level, it does not have to compete. Without competition, there is little or no pressure to provide goods or services efficiently. Because of this negligence, we need extra protection from the political system and its out-of-control abuses. The following are some activities that your government should *not* be doing:

- Making backroom deals that cost public organizations trust and dollars from overly taxed constituents
- Establishing laws or rules beyond its jurisdictional powers
- Stifling communications with its citizens
- Mismanaging money through weak or no accountability
- Being disrespectful to its citizens
- Undertaking activities that may be better served by business, families, nonprofits, or other organizations
- Establishing excessive forced taxation on its people, especially for nonpublic expenditures such as supporting charities or people in other districts

Goals are important for any organization because those who have no goals are sure to achieve it. This lack of clarity is evident at many levels of government that continue to grow beyond their original purpose. Identifying top priorities would seem to be a great first step toward slowing down the creep of more and more government for every new or expanded interest placed before the public body. For example, if families can leave an inheritance for their next generation, isn't it fair to ask government to move away from giving our children a large debt to which they are enslaved in order to repay our debts?

Though some would say it is honorable for an elected official to want to solve more and more problems with public tax dollars, one may want to ask if there are other more effective options that do not require forced taxation on a nation that is literally going broke with unsustainable debt.

Remember the principle that it is not the job of politicians to directly make our world a better place but rather to keep us free so we can individually make the world a better place in a manner that does not harm others. We must remember this premise as an overwhelming majority of Americans believe that the current political establishment is considered a failure, and seeking more of a failed government is like an alcoholic trying to drink himself sober. Most families realize that tough love, though it may be tough at first, is usually best for improving the welfare of an individual in the end. For example, the following are a few examples of how an elected official could consider solving problems. I rarely, if ever, saw these in action:

* Encourage constituents to seek help from family members, non-profits, and churches
* Recognize that elected office is necessary to maintain order, not to help friends in high places
* Identify how long a proposed solution that utilizes public taxes may take and if it is possible to establish any form of an ending or reduction
* Understand that social correctness or justice by default causes an out-of-balance list of losers
* Ask if the problem is best solved by an organization with a vested interest in fixing it or by someone who is striving to look good in his or her voting record

Private charity has become overtaken by public welfare, and the choice of citizens to support causes they believe in gets stifled. History proves that responsible, free citizens are more likely to create wealth and societal value if they are not coerced by competing forces (such as an obtrusive government). A truly free society prevents anybody from having too much power, and, frankly, America needs more competition if we are to enhance our standing within the world marketplace in many of the key areas of concern for our nation. As Thomas Jefferson once stated,

"I place economy among the first and most important virtues, and public debt as the greatest of the dangers to be feared. We must make our election between economy and liberty, or profusion and servitude."

In order to move forward as a nation, we must emphasize that politicians are not our friends; they are our entrusted fiscal managers who manage somewhere between 25 and 50 percent or more of our financial resources. To put it bluntly, this is how many self-serving politicians see us:

- As a revenue source for *their* system.
- As a vote that they crave to have power and control.
- Not as friends since what they give they must first take from someone else.
- They have less appreciation for the value of our money than most families who are living on tight budgets.
- They become more empowered by reelection to spend other people's money, often with little respect or proven ability to spend wisely.

Some of the key points of this chapter on fixing our shattered politics include:

- Demand that elected officials focus their efforts on the legitimate functions of government, which revolve around safety and security for its citizens.
- Public debt endangers our worldwide security and sustainability.
- Government spending within its means is a legitimate function, and excessive taxation or excessive spending is not.
- Americans must put pressure on each level of government to significantly curb the zeal for fiscal redistribution from federal to state to local government as this approach of governing from afar is costing our nation dearly.

- Ask elected officials to establish reasonable public goals that align with public values, including respect for marketplace limits on taxation.
- Ask elected officials to seek more proven sources of assistance for many of the social issues in America that face their constituents.

Boundaries give us a sense of our identity, and, right now,
America has few boundaries in its shattered politics.

CHAPTER 13

Demanding Transparency
and Accountability

• • •

America was intended to have a government
for the people, not for the politicians.

THIS IS *OUR* GOVERNMENT, AND we are truly entitled to know what it is doing. Unfortunately, most of us are not being told what is really going on
as more and more political elites believe that they do not need to reveal
their true actions to constituents outside of their political system. Every
governmental agency is different, but, based on my experiences directly
with local government and more indirectly with other levels; I estimate
that at least half of public decisions are made primarily in private settings.
To top it off, many of the discussions that go on in these private meetings
would disgust the taxpayers as their needs are so often irrelevant to the
decision-making processes.

Many political jurisdictions throughout the US are required to follow some form of an Open Meeting Law requirement; however, many
do not. For example, the Open Meeting Law is governed in Minnesota
by Statute 13D.01.4 which "prohibits a public body from taking a private
vote." Following is a story from our county board admitting to concur-
rence of deals before going public with a vote.

Isanti-Chisago County Star

Isanti County sets 1.7 percent levy

Becky Glander: September 15, 2009

Commissioner Alan Duff voted against the levy at the County Board meeting Sept. 15, stating he would only agree to freeze the levy. Commissioner Susan Morris was not in attendance. Sept. 15 was the deadline for setting the preliminary levy and budget.

The board voted to set the tax levy at 2 percent, claiming the increase would be mitigated slightly by new construction to make an effective levy of 1.7 percent—a total levy of $15,629,353.

The total preliminary budget of $34,985,587 was set for 2010 and approved. Duff also voted against the proposed budget.

"There's three reasons I'm not voting for this proposed tax increase," Duff said. "Before I do that I want to acknowledge that achieving a zero percent increase is very challenging, and I want to commend the board for the work getting to this point."

Duff went on to say his reasons for voting nay are that in his heart he cannot vote for a tax increase; it is a standard for his constituents – Isanti and neighboring Chisago County have voted to freeze; and "this is a poor time to raise taxes."

As was the case during a previous discussion on the levy in August, Duff was accused of "showboating" for not voting with the board.

"Mr. Duff, we sat around this board room yesterday and we all agreed--concurred—that this is what we'd do," said Commissioner

George Larson. "And now you come in with this at the last minute— it's another showboat effort on your part. The last time, I didn't jump on you for it, but this is a showboat effort. I hope the world knows it, and I'm happy to say it. I'd like to have the zero percent too."

Duff responded that there was no agreement to the levy vote at the work session the day before, because it would be illegal to make any formal decisions in closed session.

"We didn't have a formal vote, but we did sit down about it and we concurred," Larson said.

Chair Kurt Daudt said the problem with wanting a zero percent levy now is that Duff never brought any ideas to the table on how the county could do that.

"You haven't been bringing the ideas or talking about the zero percent levy to the budget meetings," he said.

"I've been talking about that since we started discussions," Duff said.

"Oh my goodness," responded Daudt. "I had to ask you in a meeting ten times where you wanted to be on the budget before you answered me, so let's not pretend you're the leader on a zero percent levy increase. In fact, it's been the opposite."[22]

The problems associated with political spin are addressed in the next chapter, but citizens are tired of elected officials making comments that are inconsistent with their actions, and their voting record. As an example, a member voting for a tax increase interestingly accuses one who voted against the tax increase of not being a leader on that issue.

In regards to the comment about *"showboating for not voting with the board,"* why would we have a board of different elected officials with different opinions if they must all unanimously agree on their votes?

Similar to parenting, where we ask our children to be honest with us, the more our children are able to take on additional responsibilities, the more tasks we give them. Right now, we generally cannot trust our politicians as they need to work hard to regain our trust as faithful servants with a genuine intent to truly serve us in a manner that is best for the public welfare. Trust has to be earned, and politicians are one of the least-trusted groups in America today, so let's shine a light on them to let them know we are watching. When they lie to us or make public decisions in private, we need to make them accountable for their actions.

It is critical that we get more informed and motivated as constituents who demand true representation of the governed by elected officials since breaking down the barriers of the political system requires constant observation and follow-through by many concerned citizens. There are many examples where public administrators have their hands tied with how they can address the abuse of funds by their elected officials when they realize that bringing up these issues could result in their own termination if they pick a politician who has more friends than enemies. That is why we the people need to ask our elected officials questions about transparency and fiduciary responsibility because it is our money that we pay in such large sums, and the insiders of the political system do not want us to know about their mistakes for numerous reasons.

A core group of concerned citizen watchdogs from the City of Victoria (Twin Cities suburb) illustrates a great example of working diligently to improve transparency with their local elected officials. Below is an excerpt from the Center of American Experiment regarding this case.

Center of the American Experiment
(A nonpartisan tax-exempt, public policy and educational institution committed to Building a Culture of Prosperity for Minnesota and the Nation.)

Landmark Ruling as Court Finds Victoria City Officials Committed 38 Open Meeting Law Violations

Tom Steward: April 1, 2016

In what may be the biggest Open Meeting law case in Minnesota history, a Carver County District Court has found four current Victoria City Council members committed a total of 38 intentional violations of the state transparency statute, leveling a total of $7,800 in personal fines.

The civil case brought by 13 residents of the Twin Cities suburb alleged numerous violations of the Open Meeting Law by city officials in 2013 in the process leading up to building a new city hall and public works building. State law requires governmental bodies to open their meetings to the public for transparency and stipulates fines of up to $300 for each intentional violation.

"They've been convicted of not complying with the law and misled the public about what was truly going on," said Tom Funk, a plaintiff with wife Carolyn. "The public was not allowed to participate in and witness the decision making process."[23]

There are many examples of how our tax dollars are often wasted on expenditures that are truly sickening and disrespectful to a society where most hardworking families live paycheck to paycheck. If the public only knew just how bad it really is, we would be watching over them like a hawk. We can watch our public tax dollars "at work" by watching governmental meetings. The best ways, in order to gain true understanding, are by attending in person, watching on television, listening to verbal recordings, and, lastly, reviewing agendas and minutes (remember that minutes legally carry motions forward but are typically very sanitized summaries of the political discourse that came to the voting conclusion).

Asking to see intergovernmental issuance of funds helps concerned citizens follow the money and identify the validity of expenditures. Remembering that many elected officials do not want to be scrutinized for their public actions, the following are some key questions to ask to help assess whether your public officials are being honest and transparent and are utilizing your tax dollars for legitimate public services.

- Ask what other organizations are supported by your tax dollars and why.
- What is its mission or the goals of the organization?
- What safeguards and auditing procedures are in place to ensure legitimate public expenditures?
- Do they have a long-term financial plan and a reasonable fund balance?
- Does the organization have a plan on how to go forward if/when intergovernmental funds are reduced and/or taken away?
- Does the organization's leadership have any commitments in writing to abide by any code of ethics or legal training in public policymaking?

In a free society, businesses can function at a high efficiency when owners responsibly supervise their employees and empower them to make good decisions that benefit the company and the clients/customers they serve. Using this analogy, our political system would work better if we watched them and asked them to make decisions that benefit its taxpayers more than their own self-serving motives, groups, and so on. When watching, be mindful that excessive amounts of unanimous votes may mean that the real debates on the issues are taking place in private settings as some opposition should be expected at times for controversial issues. It is also important to identify how the organization handles communications with its constituents.

Remember that you are viewed by many political elites as a revenue source with generally unlimited resources available for their political system. Voicing our concerns that our budgets at home are very limited and exhausted in a manner that motivates the political elite to respect those limits can bring a very significant change to the practice going on in many shattered political systems today. Just like many politicians want us to be generous in our tax giving, we have every right, as well as responsibility, to let the political elites know that we expect them to treat their requests for our limited resources with respect, transparency, and efficiency.

As Thomas Paine pointed out early on in American history, politicians will need limits on their requests; otherwise, their appetites will consume them and cost us much. With taxation out of control virtually everywhere, I believe it is reasonable to ask our elected officials to tie in maximum tax-increase limits that follow reasonable revenue sources. For example, if inflation for a state is 2 percent, and the population and commercial base are the same as the year before, it would stand to reason that taxes should not increase more than 2 percent (otherwise, this is living beyond one's means, and it needs to stop). I find it ironic that politicians call entrepreneurs and successful citizens greedy for wanting to keep their own hard-earned money, yet they do not see the hypocrisy when they think they are entitled to force us to pay them more. When articulating restraints in government spending, be sure to tie in to local market realities as well as the analogy of having to live within a budget just like families do all across America.

Public accountability could be enhanced if we require our elected officials to function using a job description with responsibilities, just like in most business settings. Ask your elected officials to commit to public service in a manner that includes integrity, honesty, and actions that demonstrate public service to others. Always follow the basic principle of following the buck as that is where most mischief takes place as far too many politicians have crafted unique ways to skim off the top from taxpayers (per diems, conferences/trips, side deals with developers, side deals for leadership in other organizations, and so on).

Public officials reading this book must always remember that transparency is critical for improving the reputation and validity of our public organizations. This was highlighted very well by Senator Jeff Sessions who made the following statement on January 16, 2014 regarding transparency with our US Senate:

"The Senate is where the great issues of our time are supposed to be examined, reviewed, and discussed before the whole nation. Yet, in the last few years, we have witnessed the dramatic erosion of Senators' rights and the dismantling of the open legislative process (...) All of us, both parties, have a responsibility to stop and reverse these trends. It's in the national interest. It's the right thing to do. All of us owe our constituents an open, deliberative process where the great issues of the day are debated in full and open public view (...) the democratic process is messy, sometimes contentious, and often difficult. But it is precisely this legislative tug of war, this back and forth, which forges national consensus. While secret deals may keep the trains running on time, they often keep them running in the wrong direction."

Some of the key points in this chapter for fixing our shattered politics are as follow:

* Transparency is essential to closing the confidence gap between political elites and outsiders to the system and must be demanded by concerned citizens from their government.
* Political elites have not earned the right to be trusted, and we should verify the legitimacy of their actions as best as possible.

* Political accountability in America will not improve until we demand it.
* Political systems should have the same level of public accountability as those steps required of its citizens (auditing, open communications, and the like).
* We need to watch our politicians like a hawk in order to bring any reasonable level of improvement to our shattered politics.

"Trust but verify!"

Ronald Reagan

CHAPTER 14

Improving Our Political Dialogue

• • •

"I have a dream that my four little children will one day
live in a nation where they will not be judged by the color
of their skin, but by the content of their character."

MARTIN LUTHER KING JR.

IT IS MY HOPE TO write this book without pointing fingers at any of our political parties or exasperating readers with an already exhausted discussion
of class warfare or racial issues. My hope is that readers will have a passion
to be responsible citizens focused on bringing America back to greatness,
no matter your political affiliation, skin color, sexual preference, financial
status, or any other designation/label that we use to pigeonhole people.
By definition, America is a true melting pot of diversity, which makes
us a very unique nation in the world. I remember embracing the value of
diversity often during my years of military service as we recognized how
different backgrounds blended together for a common goal, which often
made for a strong, cohesive unit.

Two major parties have made a significant impact on the political
landscape throughout America from local to federal levels of government.
They each have many strengths as well as weaknesses, the same as other
political parties that have evolved over time in America. Many Americans

are tired of hearing politicians go out of their way to represent the interests of their parties (namely, control) instead of the needs of their constituents for freedom and genuine public service. The one true idea worth preserving is the great American foundation of prosperity and freedom built on self-reliance and capitalistic opportunities for every person to succeed and provide value in the marketplace.

Beyond the negative ramifications associated with the excessive use of labels, many politicians have cleverly found ways to politically spin the meaning of key political words that often have no true market or cultural reality to them. For example, I know a state-elected official who claims he is conservative even though he has a lengthy record of voting for tax increases more than double the rate of inflation and who, in private meetings, complains about others being too conservative. We need to recognize that political labels are often used by slick politicians who care more about public opinion polls and about what they think you want to hear more than the reality of their actions.

Much of current American political dialogue centers around economic classifications and how to treat (e.g., tax) each class level. As President Abraham Lincoln said, "Bringing down the rich does not bring up the poor." We live in a great nation where people can, for the most part, choose to work where and when they want, and they have the capability to make a decent amount of income as they work within their God-given abilities, chosen risks, training, and initiative to make positive contributions within the marketplace. That is the blessing of a free society where, as our founding fathers so elegantly stated in our Declaration of Independence, each person has the inalienable right to pursue life, liberty, and happiness.

All citizens have a right to fair treatment, not special privilege or handouts due to various social classifications. Fair treatment can be defined within America as an opportunity, as well as a responsibility, to pursue a meaningful and happy life, not as a designation for free gifts at the expense of others who are forced to support them.

With less governmental intrusion in our lives, the human capital of America can unleash its proven potential for greatness. Freedom means giving every individual the dignity and respect equally to succeed or even fail. In fact, I would argue that failure is often a critical step toward success as the stories of many great successes by both Thomas Edison and Abraham Lincoln often began with setbacks or failures. But they both had the fortitude to learn from these mistakes and create great things for our nation. This approach thrived for over two hundred years in America, while there has been a significant decline in the economic condition of America within the world marketplace in recent years.

Today's political abuse of redistribution has gone beyond a genuine public service, and I would argue that, at least to some degree, it is part of a design to increase control of the political system more than to genuinely help others. To help illustrate how expansive entitlements have become in America, one can review benefits.gov and find that there are over six hundred entitlement programs. Providing a safety net for those in need is a kind gesture to do in any society, but isn't it fair to ask if we have exceeded a respectable safety-net level with government handouts? The value of tough love compared to government redistribution of excessive entitlements can be summarized as follows:

* Tough love instills personal pride and dignity, while redistribution takes away from the self-reliant and free spirit of mankind.
* Tough love results in creating responsible behaviors, while redistribution transfers personal responsibility to a co-enabling system.
* Tough love results in individual success through perseverance and necessity, while redistribution discourages individual success with free handouts.

◈   Tough love advances freedom for the individual to make his or her own choices, while redistribution fosters enslavement to others.

Class warfare is simply getting out of control in America. I hear so much anger and hostility toward the "evil rich," and I wonder why the jealousy has reached such a troubling level in the land of the free. Some rich people may be evil, but, then again, that same statement could be made about many other economic classes. Aren't we trying to move away from stereotyping people in today's culture? If the rich are evil, couldn't the same argument be made that politicians who want to force you to pay nearly half of what you earn are evil too? Class warfare has gone to such a high extreme in recent years, but we were warned about it over 150 years ago in some of Abraham Lincoln's most famous words of wisdom regarding the economic status of Americans.

Abraham Lincoln on the Economic Status of America

1. "You cannot bring about prosperity by discouraging thrift."
2. "You cannot strengthen the weak by weakening the strong."
3. "You cannot help small men up by tearing big men down."
4. "You cannot help the poor by destroying the rich."
5. "You cannot lift the wage-earner up by pulling the wage-payer down."
6. "You cannot keep out of trouble by spending more than your income."
7. "You cannot further the brotherhood of man by inciting class hatred."
8. "You cannot establish sound social security on borrowed money."
9. "You cannot build character and courage by taking away a man's initiative and independence."
10. "You cannot help men permanently by doing for them what they could and should do for themselves."

If we are going to use labels and terms, below are some words that are often misused in today's political communications that are rewritten in the context of a free society.

Revised Political Speak

- **Career politician.** Someone who has been able to work the system to his or her advantage while giving the impression that he or she is helping others.
- **Choice.** One of the most sought-after rights by many Americans, it is being eroded by abusive politicians that have taken over more rights and choices for Americans in their day-to-day living (such as paying more for taxes than house payments for many).
- **Civic Responsibility.** Taking care of the business of the public. Most citizens do not realize the full implications of public management on their personal lives.
- **Dream.** The ability to believe with some possibility of hope that tomorrow could be a better place for our future generations (this has severely eroded in recent years).
- **Entitlement.** The original intent in America was for citizens to be entitled to freedom and the pursuit of happiness, but that has grown significantly in recent decades to include items such as health care, college education, cell phones and more.
- **Freedom.** The ability to act independently of excessive or abusive government rules or financial restraints in a manner that is not detrimental to others in society (opposite of "free dumb," which is the pressure to be silent in the face of tyranny).
- **Gratitude.** Choosing to appreciate the blessings that are abundantly all around us in America instead of complaining that we do not have as much as our neighbors.
- **Honorable Public Service.** Elected officials who serve the public for public benefit, including respectable consideration of the limits

on forced taxation. They attempt to vote based on their best judgment based on independent evaluations over the merits of an issue without undue influence by special interests, personal considerations or system-insider payoffs.

* **Tough love.** Genuine concern and encouragement for a person's long-term well-being, which allows natural consequences to occur as a disciplinary opportunity for teaching instead of protecting individuals from negative but necessary outcomes.
* **Political elite.** Elected officials who are more focused on personal power than serving the public. They tend to think they are better than others and vote primarily based on influences from political insiders which help them get re-elected and continue to grow the internal political system.
* **Power.** Was originally designed to be held by the citizens of America, but is now held by the political elite.
* **Sacrifice.** Willingness to serve the public good more than personal interests (such as the military, firefighters, police and so on).
* **Self-reliance.** A key value to the foundation of America where citizens take personal responsibility for one's self while demanding less government.
* **US Constitution.** A strongly written document that established freedom and liberty for an exceptional and unique nation.

Some of the key points from this chapter are as follow:

* Labels and designations can be dangerous as they stereotype people unfairly or are used for purposes of gaining political power.
* Definitions used by politicians often do not correlate with market or social realities.
* Some qualities that were once respected and admired in America have been revised into negative qualities, and we need to modify our political dialogue.

* Abraham Lincoln summed up the problems of class warfare over 150 years ago in a way that is still very relevant today.
* America has an over two-hundred-year history of prosperity that succeeded based on strong entrepreneurship and hard work.

"In normal life we hardly realize how much more we receive than we give, and life cannot be rich without such gratitude. It is so easy to overestimate the importance of our own achievements compared with what we owe to the help of others."

DIETRICH BONHOEFFER, LETTERS AND PAPERS FROM PRISON

CHAPTER 15

Bring It on Home

• • •

*The challenge is to help people see the benefits of limited government
and to recognize the costs of unlimited government.*

In order to motivate greater citizen involvement in fixing our shattered politics, we must be able to explain how political decisions impact the individual and family in a more personal manner. Most people have no clear understanding what a national debt of $19 trillion means to them personally until it can be explained as a fifty-six-thousand-dollar burden for every American. I was born into a relatively poor working-class family, but my parents never saddled me with debts as an inheritance like our government has done to all of us. When attempting to grasp the concept of this massive debt and out-of-control government spending, you should remember a few things:

* National debt numbers are overwhelming, and it affects all of us by weakening the prosperity and security of our nation.
* When adding up personal tax liabilities, it is important to remember all taxes paid to all taxing authorities throughout the year (virtually everyone knows if they are paying into or receiving funds from the federal government in mid-April each year; however, few of us know how much we pay in total taxes throughout the year).
* Recognize that corporate income taxes paid by American businesses are taxed at one of the highest rates in the world.

* Asking for more regulations adversely impacts many people (there are almost always losers as well as winners in every political decision).
* Once started, government programs rarely go away and cost both current and future generations.

Do you cut things in your personal budget at home? I would be willing to bet that nearly every reader of this book will answer that question with a yes, at least at some point in his or her life. Yet, that very rarely happens in government; as Ronald Reagan once said, the closest thing we have to eternal life in America is a government program. My experience with budgeting at Isanti County and at several federal levels was just to keep doing the same thing and add somewhere between 3–5 percent for inflation every year while rarely asking if there may be a more efficient way of providing this service. The following are a few key examples of America's public finance situation that bring home the message at different levels of our shattered politics:

* Taxes, along with house payments, represent one of the highest monthly line-item costs to the average family.
* Our 2015 federal budget of $3.8 trillion results in an average tax burden of approximately one thousand dollars per month for each person in the US.
* The average state taxes in 2015 were $5,642 per person, with a low of $2,993 in Alaska to a high of $7,719 in Illinois.
* Local tax liabilities vary significantly by jurisdiction but typically average about 20 percent of our overall taxes (about two to four thousand dollars per year).

Americans are blessed with significant resources, including an economy that is the envy of the world. Yes, we have problems like everyone else, but we also have many more financial resources than most nations. We have worked hard to earn these resources, and we deserve a government that respects that hard work and spends these resources with thoughtful diligence. Virtually all Americans I know spend a significant amount of time managing their primary financial obligations, including categories like house payments/rents, vehicle loans, retirement accounts, medical insurances, children and schooling, and recreational activities. However, most Americans spend minimal time reviewing one of their most expensive categories, their taxes. Most Americans look closely at tax obligations during the first few weeks of April and then move on to other priorities after taxes are paid on the fifteenth. But if taxes are arguably one of our highest financial obligations alongside housing, isn't that an area we should spend at least some time reviewing to assess how it can be better? I realize politics is not as exciting as most of these other items, but, believe me, it is just as costly and deserves our attention as citizens if it is to ever improve (unless you think that the current political elite are going to fix it).

I believe that part of the challenge that overwhelms most concerned citizens is that our government is now such a large problem that it is hard to know where to identify the most critical areas where good-hearted people can help make a positive difference. Government has covered up the problem by taking it further away from the taxpayer so that more shenanigans can be done from a greater distance at taxpayers' expense. In order to better understand the value of a smaller government, we must also recognize the intrinsic value it creates beyond the dollar.

* Hard workers making an honest buck by doing an honest job feel personal pride in being able to keep a fair portion of their pay.
* Risk takers leveraging personal assets with the hopes of starting a small business get fairly compensated for their risks and perseverance.
* Lower taxes increase the opportunity for citizens to give freely to others as they choose, not as forced by a political system.
* Citizens can save for retirement and set aside an inheritance for the next generation without government asking for one more handout via death taxes.

♦ The vast confidence gap between politician and citizen is reduced when citizens see their taxes used for local programs or services with known and effective results rather than being used for improper or faraway purposes.

I applaud one of our county commissioners in Minnesota who contacted me asking for help finding a disabled veteran who might be interested in a new home donated by various charities. At our initial meeting, I asked him why he was asking me to help him when he had a veteran service officer who worked for him at the county he governed. His answer was insightful; he said he wanted the job done right by a person with a passion for helping disabled veterans and proven effectiveness in getting the job done right. Several weeks later, we found a homeless disabled veteran and his pregnant wife, and we were able to provide them with a car, job, and home. This is an exciting story of thinking outside the normal box of government solutions and identifying nonprofit sources that are more vested in the issue and can solve it at *no* cost to the taxpayer. In addition, this exciting story continues as we held a baby shower and were blessed with many anonymous gifts generously dropped off for the couple at our front door, including a computer donated from a local business. Below is a picture of this young disabled veteran and his pregnant wife at the groundbreaking ceremony for their new home.

**Picture of Disabled Veteran and Pregnant Wife at
New Home Groundbreaking Ceremony**

The further removed that taxpayers are from their taxes; the less likely it is that there will be a recognized value for that service. That is why the US governing system was designed to be concentrated at the local level, where local citizens can be more engaged, sense the impacts of their public taxes, and voice appreciation or concerns with elected officials who serve closer to the constituents they serve. American citizens need to be able to express their distaste for political redistribution from higher levels of government to lower levels because it:

* Separates the investment from the value
* Exacerbates the growth and interdependence of more government
* Replaces other structures that may work better
* Sets up false pretenses of problem solving that are not sustainable
* Causes us to simply run out of other people's money

Americans value choice, but, in recent years, our government has taken or is considering taking away some of our choices that we used to value so much, such as:

* Ability to choose our own doctors and healthcare coverage
* Ability to express ourselves as protected by our First Amendment right without concerns about political correctness
* Ability to bear arms in accordance with our Second Amendment right
* Ability to donate our own funds to charities we want, free of taxes
* Ability to express displeasure over an abusive government
* Ability to view expenditures of our public tax dollars

The US federal tax burden alone equates to almost twelve thousand dollars every year for every woman, man, and child in the United States (about one thousand dollars per month). That is a serious expenditure of funds that should be evaluated and honestly debated by the taxpayers and the elected officials who are spending our tax dollars. One way for

American families to grasp the vast differences in priorities between their budgets and the budgets of most shattered politics is to look at the general priorities of each unit. Though there are obviously many exceptions, some typical family values contrast with today's common political values are illustrated in Table 4.

Table 4
Typical Family Values versus Political Values

American Families	versus	Politicians
Equal opportunities for all		Class warfare and equal outcomes
Competition and free enterprise		Power and control
Real budgets often with cuts		No budgets, and cuts are infrequent
Supporting our children		Support the political system
Direct, open, and honest		Sneaky, elusive, and irresponsible
Practical and efficient (reality-based)		Utopian and experimental
Acquiring materials by producing		Taking materials from producers
Debt manageable for most		Out of control & unsustainable debt
Raising children to be independent		Increasing citizens' dependence

Some of the key points from this chapter are as follow:

* Remind others within your sphere that government is technically incapable of caring about your well-being more than family, friends, or other associated groups.

* Most families and businesses cut items in their budgets on a regular basis, but this rarely happens in today's shattered politics.
* Taxes, along with house payments, represent one of the highest monthly line-item costs to the average family, and investing more energy in understanding and overseeing this cost is critical for our nation's future.
* The US federal government has given us a $19-trillion debt, a burden of fifty-six thousand dollars for every man, woman, and child in our country.
* Our 2015 federal budget of $3.8 trillion results in an average tax burden of approximately one thousand dollars per month for each person in the nation.
* Average state taxes in 2015 were $5,642 per person with a low of $2,993 in Alaska to a high of $7,719 in Illinois.
* Local tax liabilities vary significantly by jurisdiction but typically average about 20 percent of our overall tax liabilities (about two to four thousand dollars per year).
* Excessive government rule takes away many of our choices and freedoms.

"Government exists to protect us from each other. Where government has gone beyond its limits is in deciding to protect us from ourselves."

RONALD REAGAN

CHAPTER 16

Bringing Corporate Best Practices into the Political System

• • •

Incorporating some of the best practices and principles from the
private sector could help improve our shattered politics.

IN ORDER FOR A BUSINESS to survive, it must make a return on its invest-ment or, in other words, pay the expenses with received revenues. In order to effectively do this, business owners frequently assess what works and what isn't, including employee performances and other tangible assets. There are few similar performance indicators for the performance of gov-ernment programs, and thus ideas get bigger although results too often do not follow. In other words, it is far too common for politicians to focus about 95 percent of their efforts on the problem (demands) and 5 percent of their efforts on the limits and reasonable concerns of the taxpaying constituents (costs). We need a better balance that respects the problems created by over-taxation.

Businesses start when entrepreneurial leaders identify a problem or need and take risks with upfront investments of time and money to cre-ate a product or service that fill that need. The business then grows when owners hire employees and provide them with tasks and responsibilities. Strong companies ensure that employees have the reasonable resources available to meet their goals, and their value to the organization is typically assessed using some form of measurable results. There is an accountability standard, whether formal or informal, built within companies that ensures that valued products or services are created. In government, there is minimal evaluation of value other than general perceptions of trying to please the most active constituents. Wouldn't it be nice if government had the business tools to evaluate which programs are working and which ones are not and, most importantly, have the power to fix those problems that are not working? Taxpayers would benefit from this accountability, and it would help bring the forgotten taxpayer closer to the political system to help identify best management practices available to the public.

A publicly declared code of ethics can help improve an industry's acceptance into the marketplace if it is established, adhered to, and monitored by stakeholders. For example, one of the most respected professions according to recent Gallup polls is pharmacists. Professional pharmacists are guided by the following code, which publicly states the principles that form the fundamental basis of the roles and responsibilities of pharmacists based on moral obligations and virtues. These principles include the following points:

* A pharmacist respects the covenantal relationship between the patient and pharmacist.
* A pharmacist promotes the good of every patient in a caring, compassionate, and confidential manner.
* A pharmacist respects the autonomy and dignity of each patient.
* A pharmacist acts with honesty and integrity in professional relationships.
* A pharmacist maintains professional competence.
* A pharmacist respects the values and abilities of colleagues and other health professionals.
* A pharmacist serves individual, community, and societal needs.
* A pharmacist seeks justice in the distribution of health resources.[24]

Other examples of codes of ethics found in other respected public-service industries include ethical principles such as:

* Honesty and fairness demonstrated by professional personal conduct
* Raising the standards of excellence within the profession whenever possible
* Pursuing relationships and activities based on honesty and fairness
* Upholding all laws, policies, and regulations of the organization
* Striving to meet the highest ethical standards and report unethical behaviors
* Supporting the rights of others without discriminating
* Loyalty to pursuing objectives that are consistent with the public interest

Embracing solid principles that show the marketplace that an organization will serve its customers in an ethical, fair, and professional manner will gain respect from citizens and help break down barriers between buyers and sellers in the marketplace. The Better Business Bureau (BBB) was founded in 1912 as a nonprofit organization focused on advancing marketplace trust. It promotes principles within the marketplace to help businesses establish and maintain trust based on these exceptional principles of trust.

* Build trust: establish and maintain a positive track record in the marketplace.
* Advertise honestly: adhere to established standards of advertising and selling.
* Tell the truth: honestly represent products and services, including clear and adequate disclosures of all material terms.
* Be transparent: openly identify the nature, location, and ownership of the business, and clearly disclose all policies, guarantees, and procedures that bear on a customer's decision to buy.

- Honor promises: abide by all written agreements and verbal representations.
- Be responsive: address marketplace disputes quickly, professionally, and in good faith.
- Safeguard privacy: protect any data collected against mishandling and fraud, collect personal information only as needed, and respect the preferences of consumers regarding the use of their information.
- Embody integrity: Approach all business dealings, marketplace transactions, and commitments with integrity.[25]

In the minds of many Americans, most politicians today would likely receive a failing score in most if not all of these categories. If America's elected officials could improve their scores in these key trust areas to a more respectable level, our appreciation of this profession would improve, our nation would be much better off, and our future would be more promising. Following are several examples I have seen where local government has established business practices that enhanced public value for their constituents:

- Establish goals and budgets based on marketplace realities.
- Define tasks and the most efficient way(s) to accomplish the tasks within reasonable fiscal limitations.
- Establish an internal Code of Ethics and punish violations internally to preserve the integrity of the organization.
- Cut programs that are outdated or modify those which provide a poor return-on-investment.

Corporate America knows how to create value for its customers and even make a profit when its revenues exceed its costs. Governmental accounting and taxation are difficult for many to understand. Personally, I believe that much of the detail that complicates some aspects of public finance is designed to overwhelm the average person, who can no longer follow the trail of money in public circles. But the fundamentals of public finance are really not much different than those of personal, family, or business finance. The primary difference is that the public sector has no real ramifications for spending beyond its means (businesses have to receive enough revenues to pay costs, or they go out of business, and families have to manage family budgets, or they lose assets). Many public finance systems lack detailed mechanisms in place to identify the specific uses or values of their expenditures. I believe that some political organizations withhold this information for a very solid reason: they know that there would be an uproar if citizens knew that their tax dollars were going to other geographic regions or to issues they do not want to support.

Some of the key points from this chapter for fixing our shattered politics are as follow:

* We need to demand that elected officials evaluate costs and sustainability as much as, if not more than, the exaggerated value of their proposed solutions that warrant our hard-earned taxpaying money.
* The Better Business Bureau oversees business ethics and promotes integrity based on great virtues that could be a useful guideline for improving the trust levels between concerned citizens and our public officials.
* A code of ethics is a common tool that is rigidly enforced within many respected professions but is largely absent within most political systems and is generally not enforced where it may be in place (the rules of genuine service are often not abided by many political elites).
* The political system as a whole fails in abiding by many business principles that promote integrity and other related trust qualities.
* Accountability for public expenditures has become complicated with multiple layers of subsistence, and bringing the true costs of

public services closer to local government will help taxpayers see the real cost, as well as value, of their tax dollars at work.

"The time is always right to do what is right."

MARTIN LUTHER KING

CHAPTER 17

Bringing Military Principles
into the Political System

• • •

Service doesn't end...Freedom isn't Free.

-Concerned Veterans for America

America's great military is fundamentally based on accountability to others and depending on everyone to pull his or her weight. Military leaders train their soldiers to know who they are, where they are, and what the standards are for the situations they are engaged in. If you do not pull your weight, the consequences are high as lives become endangered. This mind-set of ever-present accountability would be nice to apply to politicians as the analogy is real, and the life of America is in serious jeopardy.

Our brave military members who willingly fight for something greater than themselves provide us with an example of how a high degree of safety and freedom can be achieved through much sacrifice and noble service. The military by and large is comprised of fighters who bond together in very unique ways to overcome many adversities. Conversely, politicians are a group of very strong fighters for what they believe in—namely, themselves and their power circles. We need more people who are sacrificial servants in public service instead of the group of self-serving politicians who currently rule much of our shattered politics.

Our military veterans arguably represent one of our biggest political stakeholders in our nation as they have already invested much sacrifice for our freedoms. It has been very disheartening for me to speak with so many honorable military members who have come home in recent years to a nation that is losing its pride and distinction as the pinnacle of a place to live and raise a family. On a side note, it is even more frustrating when these brave men and women overseas often cannot be given an opportunity to vote and have their ballots counted, even though they arguably have the most on the line to win or lose with the political system that identifies how, where, and when we are to fight for the defense of our nation.

Veterans know the cost of freedom as it is driven home during basic training, and service members take pride in fighting for a cause greater than themselves. Military service members also learn personal responsibility and how to make groups stronger by identifying individual strengths from diverse Americans and blending these differences together for the best group outcome. As an enlisted soldier in the US Army, I had a job to do to the best of my abilities and follow my chain of command. As an officer, I quickly learned the importance of pushing tasks downhill. This same concept can apply to politics as we chip away at the power of the federal government by bringing the power of expenditures down to the smallest governmental units that are closest to the needs of the people and, frankly, where accountability is easier to manage.

Soldiers fully grasp the concept of selfless sacrifice. These sacrifices include time away from family, minimal pay, potential of putting their lives on the line, and much more. On the other hand, far too many politicians are more interested in their own motives, personal power, or easy money (it's sad how some complain publicly about their "low pay" while laughing privately about how it was the easiest way to make a buck). America's shattered politics can improve if we could incorporate a few of the key principles of our first-class military organization, including the following steps:

- Recruit quality people who are motivated to serve others.
- Train them on basics of the job and the importance of integrity.
- Empower them to embrace strong public-service principles over personal considerations.
- Recognize the value of establishing goals and standards.
- Instill that it is an honor to serve others, not a bully pulpit or career position.
- Discharge those who do deliberately illegal acts.

Fundamentally, the number-one job of an elected official in America is to protect the citizens and maintain a safe place to live, work, and play. This role of protection obviously includes overseeing a military for national and international defense, a homeland security department for national security, and other aspects of security, including protection of our vital resources. An extended aspect of national security is protecting us against wrongdoings from and excessive obligations to other nations, which can jeopardize our role as a strong nation.

The military code of conduct is a six-article code that provides general guidelines for the daily conduct of all US military personnel. It is especially applicable during times of war or imprisonment. Living by this code requires a great deal of sacrifice and commitment, as our soldiers know all too well, yet they still eagerly accept the challenge. I believe that these principles can be adopted to help better ensure that our elected officials serve us instead of their internal political system. For example, this code of conduct could be paraphrased to guide elected officials in such a way:

- I am an elected official of XYZ and am dedicated to serving my constituents to the best of my abilities.
- I will never stop advocating for fairness and conscientious management of the finite resources entrusted to my governance.

* I will not take bribes or any special favors, real or perceived, from any special-interest groups in performing my duties.
* I will faithfully executive the responsibilities of my position and respect the limited resources of the citizens I represent.
* I will try to make my jurisdiction better than it was before I leave this temporary position.
* I recognize that it is my responsibility is to preserve the freedom and security of the people I represent and not to force any actions that reduce these freedoms.

Perhaps the strongest place where there is little room for blaming others is in the military, where orders are given through a chain of command and are closely followed by disciplined soldiers, or else they face severe punishment for failing to comply with lawful orders. Through intense training, soldiers quickly learn that their mistakes can cost the lives of others, thus they quickly buy in to group solutions for their unit's welfare and safety. Soldiers buy into this concept because they have to as part of the safeguard of military service, but they also do so willingly because they share a common bond of helping with the overall mission (defense of our nation). In politics, there are very rarely any common goals such as love for country, patriotism, or others that bring politicians together, and when there are primary interests expressed by the public, they are too often cast aside by some elected officials for personal goals or agendas rather than genuine public service that benefit the public.

Freedom is not free; it is purchased through much sacrifice and very hard work—just ask any brave military member of our great nation who sacrificed much for this freedom. Freedom cannot be kept without a real, strong, sustained effort that overcomes the mess we have created by allowing an out-of-control government to spiral so far down that recovery seems almost unreachable.

Some of the key points from this chapter are as follow:

- Our military veterans have arguably sacrificed the most to defend the freedom of our great nation, and their unique training and discipline make many of them candidates to bring these respectable qualities to help improve our shattered politics.
- The fundamental role of our elected officials is to protect the people it governs, a responsibility similar to one that has been respectfully performed by our brave men and women in military uniform.
- The military code of conduct can be modified to help establish a higher level of conduct for our politicians.
- Our military is highly respected as a place of exceptional public service, and our shattered politics would improve by incorporating many of its principles.

"I've lived the literal meaning of the land of the free and home of the brave. It's not corny for me. I feel it in my heart."

CHRIS KYLE, AMERICAN SNIPER

CHAPTER 18

Hit the Road, Jack—a Case for Term Limits

• • •

If an overwhelming majority of Americans do not respect or approve of the job of their politicians, wouldn't it make sense to bring term limits to political offices besides the presidential office?

Term limits are a necessary instrument to help curb the level of corruption and transition the focus of elected office to public service rather than personal power. The rationale for term limits extends beyond the presidential office. Enacting term limits with other elected offices would result in fresh, new ideas instead of the old-school, stale ideas that have not been effective or appreciated by the public in recent decades. Besides, when something is shattered as badly as our political landscape currently is, doesn't it make sense to put the pieces back together with new leadership?

The political elite are ruining the American dream, and citizens have not only the right but the responsibility as well to become involved in helping to fix this problem. Career politicians have become the ruling elite, and few of us are happy with their leadership, so we need a strong boost of citizen-led initiatives to enact more term limits across the political spectrum if we are going to improve this situation. Many elected officials have made millions of dollars off the taxpayers of our nation through playing the game of politics for ten, twenty, and even more than forty years. The founding fathers did not intend for politics to be a career position as there are so many insidious abuses that take place by many politicians who abuse the system for their own favor.

In addition to the original intent of the American political system designed in the eighteenth century, Americans recognized the value of term limits in 1951, when we enacted presidential term limits. Then several states added term limits beginning in 1990 (thirty-five states now have term limits for the office of governor). Though term limits were established for the office of president and several state-elected positions across the United States, US Congress and many other elected office positions have no term limits. Congress members and many other state and local levels of politicians have worked hard to stay in office for many terms because of pay raises, health and retirement benefits, and the intoxication of power. The movement to term limits has helped curb this appetite within a few offices, and with the current shattered political situation, it is time to instill additional term limits in other political offices where abuses are destroying our once-great nation.

Congress has an approval rating of less than 10 percent, but its members are reelected 90 percent of the time across the nation. Does this make sense to you? (Ironically, these out-of-balance numbers also apply to many state-level elected offices.) This means that the politicians have been successful in fooling the voters, and it also underscores how our shattered politics will not improve without real change initiated by concerned citizens. We have a responsibility as citizens to demand change to this abusive system, and term limits help alleviate some of the problems of a stale, power-driven system that is not valued by an overwhelming majority of Americans today.

Once in the political system, far too many elected officials become more dangerous to the citizens who voted them into office. Have you ever heard "I liked a lot of what candidate X said before s/he was elected? Now s/he seems to be motivated by other factors different than what was promised during the campaign."? Well, that is because there are other factors that influence politicians more once they are in office—much more. For example, we currently have a large political party in flux as party insiders feel their opinions should shape the nomination process more than the concerned citizens who took time to vote in primaries and caucuses. Citizens, we have lost our country to the political elite, and we the people need to take it back.

Beyond working within their own political jurisdictions, politicians also work with other politicians from within other political boundaries within the same voting district to garner additional inside favors. Some of this can be good as it is certainly understandable for politicians from different boundaries to get along, but when the purpose is more about power and reelection than genuine public service, citizens once again lose out to the power game of insider politics. Career politicians typically become more focused on building internal connections with other politicians and focus less on public service and diligence to effectively manage the resources entrusted to them by constituents. Too often, we vote for recognized names on the ballot, and term limits can at least unravel some of these negative patterns.

Another technique used by politicians to gain an upper hand in being reelected is helping other political office holders for many reasons, including many that would be considered illegal or immoral in the "real world." For example, several watchdog groups have observed county commissioners actively campaigning for an auditor within their same county to help themselves gain further political influence and future votes. Most concerned citizens recognize the injustice of this and see it as a strong conflict of interest, but these types of questionable endeavors happen far too often in politics, and they increase the problems as politicians focus more on keeping and increasing their power rather than serving their constituents.

Just looking at this conflict of interest, one would think, *who's truly watching over the taxpayers' money when county commissioners collaborate with their own auditors to manage public resources?*

Unfortunately, the above incident did happen and is happening all around the United States in other related scenarios. The internal support of politicians helping each other leads to numerous conflicts of interest and situations where legal or moral obligations to serve constituents are often in jeopardy. With term limits in place, this kind of unethical behavior would likely reduce as candidates would be more focused on serving their constituents for their defined period of time rather than constantly working with other political insiders in preparation for re-election.

There are some arguments against term limits, and I can respect those arguments, but let's look at a few of the main objections to term limits.

- Loss of organizational knowledge and/or stability: Though there may be some truth to this, I believe that the argument for fresh, new ideas that help transition shattered politics toward some form of respectability is better.
- It could make Congress weaker: I would argue that it would result in a general transfer of base of operation from Washington, DC, to the local places that our representatives represent, thus bringing political power from the incestuous power game in DC closer to the citizens that government represents across the nation.
- Limits political choice for voters: Ironically, term limits have been demonstrated to improve choice and diversity in elections as they foster greater opportunities for others to step up and have a voice in the future of our nation.

Some of the key points from this chapter for fixing our shattered politics are as follow:

* Term limits have been enacted for the office of president, and the idea has gained traction with some state and local governmental offices throughout the United States.
* With an incumbent approval rating of about 10 percent and a re-election rate of 90 percent, it seems logical that we may want to modify our system to help limit the negative impacts associated with career politicians.
* Politicians helping other politicians with campaigns to maintain the political system's status quo are very common and bring with it numerous immoral, illegal, or questionable considerations that detract from genuine public service.
* Term limits change the political culture from one of power and control within a system to a more service-orientated one with constituents.
* Term limits would be beneficial at many levels outside of US Congress and are not likely to be implemented without significant public pressure.

"Hit the road, Jack!"

RAY CHARLES

CHAPTER 19

No More Mr. Nice Guy

• • •

*"What country can preserve its liberties if its rulers are not warned
from time to time that their people preserve the spirit of resistance?"*

CHAD GRILLS, ARMY INFANTRY VETERAN

AND AUTHOR OF SEVERAL BOOKS

AMERICANS CAN NO LONGER IDLY stand by and tolerate a morally corrupt, fiscally irresponsible political system that dismantles our nation from within. We owe that commitment to preserving freedom to those who sacrificed so much to keep our nation free and safe during troubled times like WWI and WWII. We owe that to those within our communities and to our next generation so that they are granted the same privileges and responsibilities that have been a blessing to so many throughout the history of America. Until we the people identify and support genuine leaders and statesmen and -women who truly represent our interests, we can expect a continued downward spiral and deterioration of government trust and ongoing governmental expansion into every aspect of our lives in a way that results in the rapid falling of a once-mighty nation.

In order to respectfully voice concerns over further government intrusion into our lives, it is helpful to review a few reasons why America's politics have become so shattered.

- An increase in class warfare from some wanting more government programs now at the expense of future debt to our nation and our next generation.
- A growing belief that the politician cares about their personal welfare more than other groups that have historically filled that role (such as family, church, and the like).
- An increase in the number of citizens who view the benefits of more government programs as higher than the costs associated with inefficient programs.
- A lackadaisical attitude and reduced respect toward the value of liberty and freedom as Americans distance themselves from the principles established by our founding fathers.
- A transitional belief in the typical American view that freedom comes from government and not from our Creator.
- A larger influx of citizens from other nations who are more familiar with government being the primary power structure of a nation.

America needs a stronger backbone to stand up against politicians who partake in illegal or immoral activities that are not tolerated in general society. The double standard that is so common with many of the political elite is dangerous within a free society. Unfortunately, too many bully politicians have established a poor reputation for doing whatever they can get away with, and they keep pushing the boundaries until they meet resistance. So let's resist by establishing reasonable boundaries. If our elected officials do something illegal or highly immoral, they should receive punishments just like the rest of us do in the real world. We must be vigilant and strive toward improving the political system by ensuring compliance with basic principles such as those below:

- Stealing is not tolerated as publicly acceptable behavior.
- Money is managed carefully and respectfully.
- Bribes and payouts are unacceptable, with severe punishment penalties.

* Conflicts of interest are avoided or disclosed.
* They are held accountable for lies and distortions since actions speak louder than words.

We can become more influential, concerned citizens by utilizing more direct communications with our elected officials. The acronym RATS can be used to help guide concerned citizens in our communications with our elected officials as we ask them to deliver, not just promise, the following:

* Results, not just empty promises
* Accountability that they will follow through with their commitments
* Transparency that they will be honest and candid with us
* Service—we will be served faithfully to the best of their abilities throughout their office terms, not just during election time

Concerned citizens should diligently and carefully post the truth about political abuses in various social media circles. Please do this with respect for the position and person while shining a light on the discrepancies that other constituents need to hear. Remember the basic premise is that our current political establishment is shattered or highly inefficient, and asking for more of it is akin to asking an alcoholic to drink more alcohol to get sober. Be sure to thank elected officials if they shut down an inefficient program or remove outdated services from public expenditures. We need to speak boldly to politicians and ask them to spread our work ethic instead of our wealth.

Concerned citizens must show up at public meetings and let politicians know that they are watching. Neighborhood watchdog groups can be established with those who hold similar political concerns to share responsibilities for attending political meetings and reporting the problems firsthand rather than secondhand. We must proactively protect citizens who protest wrongdoings that can have a negative impact on organizational well-being. Whistle blowing can reveal serious problems within an organization, and all public stakeholders are hurt if these are not dutifully addressed by the public entity and possibly even by concerned citizens such as was done in Clark County, Illinois (as discussed earlier in this book).

Concerned citizens need to boldly share that we no longer need or want any more "free" stuff from government as the real price is simply too high (lost freedom, low return on investment, paying system elites, and so forth). There is no free lunch. We need courageous leaders to take on entitlements and transition our mind-set back to one of self-reliance. Santa Claus is a great story for our children, but tax revenues are not an endless stream of money. "The government will eventually run out of someone else's money," as the late Margaret Thatcher so elegantly stated.

Some of the key points from this chapter are as follows:

- We cannot afford to quietly sit by as our nation falls apart from within due to a shattered political system.
- Forced taxation and redistribution is endangering America's prosperity and citizens need to bring this to the attention of their elected officials often.
- Small local watchdog groups can work together to take turns attending local political meetings and improve public accountability.
- Bully politicians are pushing the limits of acceptable tactics, and it is time for citizens to push back in a respectable and strong manner by demanding political decision-making processes include boundaries that help get our nation back on a better track of self-reliance.

> *"Silence in the face of evil is itself evil: God will not hold us guiltless. Not to speak is to speak. Not to act is to act."*
>
> DIETRICH BONHOEFFER (1939)

CHAPTER 20

Conclusion

• • •

"The true soldier fights not because he hates what is in front
of him, but because he loves what is behind him."

G. K. CHESTERTON

AMERICANS VALUE FREEDOM, LIBERTY, AND choice, but these values are currently being held hostage by a political system that provides value for very few—namely, the political elite. It is time for Americans to hold an internal fight to regain our nation, which has been lost to a political system that cares very little about the people. Our nation is designed for citizens to regain this power, but we must fight for that responsibility now, or the downward spiral of continued corruption and eroding freedoms will result in a hole too deep to get out of. Some would argue that this hole is already too deep, and there may be some truth to that. However, with the incredible history Americans have in overcoming tremendous adversity, I believe we have the opportunity and responsibility to bring back the nation of freedom and liberty that was fought for bravely by many men and women before us.

The purpose of this book is to highlight the serious challenge facing America with our current political situation, identify reasonable solutions that could help turn the tide of this destruction based on principles utilized by our military and other respected professions, and help readers identify areas where they can help. This book is not intended to be a comprehensive manual of answers to fixing our entire political system but, rather, a start toward putting the pieces of our shattered politics back together on the road to recovery.

Perhaps it is time we put a price tag on the value of freedom to help determine just how much effort we should be making to take our country back from an out-of-touch political system. For me, the value of freedom ranks right up there after my faith in God and my love for my family. I realize that the value of freedom may be hard to quantify for some, but for those who have served in our US military, we know that the price to ensure freedom is high, very high.

Politics used to be, could be, and should be a noble profession of public service, not an industry of buying favors at the expense of others. For those public servants who truly serve others with genuine hearts bent on public service, thank you. For those who are in it for self-serving motives, the concerned citizens of our great nation will be watching you as we fight to bring America back to a mighty and strong nation that is ready for another 240 years of excellence.

It is with a humble reflection on the great honor we have as Americans that I encourage each of you to urgently take the steps necessary to bring back a political system that serves us in a respectable manner so that our children and future generations will be given the great opportunity to live in a nation of freedom and prosperity for many more years to come.

God bless America, and thank you for taking the time to read this book. Let's work courageously as concerned citizens to bring the United States back to greatness as a nation that provides a shining light of hope within our oftentimes dark world.

"Land of the free and home of the brave!"

Closing line of America's national anthem

Appendix

• • •

Aꜰᴛᴇʀ ʙᴇɪɴɢ ᴛᴏʟᴅ ʙʏ ᴀ county commissioner at a work session in July 2012 that he would never support disabled veterans as long as I lived in the county, I have made it my personal mission to:

1) humbly pray for politicians that they will improve their under-standing of the incredible sacrifices made by our military service members so that they can be safe and free;
2) shine a light on politicians who do not support the brave men and women who sacrifice so much to defend our nation to help instill some accountability for their detrimental views towards the pro-tection of our nation;
3) proactively support nonprofit organizations that are committed to helping veterans in need.

In honor of our veterans, I am pleased to donate a portion of the pro-ceeds from the sale of this book to two nonprofit veteran organizations that I have worked with and that I believe have the vision, mission, and commitment to help improve the lives of our honorable veterans.

* **Honor Flight Twin Cities (www.HonorFlightTwinCities.org)**

Honor Flight Twin Cities is a 501(c) (3) nonprofit organization created solely to honor America's World War II and Korean War veterans for all of their sacrifices. This organization transports our heroes to Washington, DC, to visit and reflect at their memorials. For the veterans, and also for the guardian volunteers who go along, it is a life-changing day that has been described by many veterans as the greatest day of their lives. This incredible program is offered free of charge to veterans since the organization believes that these honorable heroes have already paid enough with their services to America. Since 2008, Honor Flight Twin Cities has taken 1,360 WWII veterans and 1,085 guardians to Washington, DC, to visit their memorials.

The program operates on donations from organizations and individuals under the shared 501 (c) (3) nonprofit umbrella of the Minnesota Vietnam Veterans Charity. Honor Flight Twin Cities is operated under the leadership of Jerry Kyser; US Army combat disabled Vietnam veteran and recipient of the prestigious 2016 Ellis Island Medal of Honor.

* **Veterans Journey Home (www.JourneyHomeMN.org)**

Veterans Journey Home is a nonprofit organization founded by Blake Huffman that is committed to working with disabled military veterans and their families with a goal of providing permanent supportive housing and helping to rebuild the lives of these military heroes. With recognition that there are often underlying issues affecting the abilities of our disabled veterans to integrate back into society and regain their productivity and self-worth, Veterans Journey Home is designed to help with this post-service journey. The guiding principles of Veterans Journey Home include:

* Sustainability—a highly personalized and unique financial model that is sensitive to each service member's financial capabilities
* Service—strengthens community involvement where volunteers gain professional experience while working on a noble cause
* Success—personal empowerment through the pride of home ownership

This organization has built six housing units with plans of adding ten more throughout Minnesota in 2016. All veteran housing projects are built or adapted to be in full compliance with the Americans with Disabilities Act. Journey Home Minnesota is the parent 501(c) (3) nonprofit organization with a mission of providing affordable housing in safe neighborhoods served by great schools to domestic-violence survivors, military veterans, and their families.

> *"Some people live an entire lifetime and wonder if they have ever made*
> *a difference in the world. A veteran doesn't have that problem."*

RONALD REAGAN

BIBLIOGRAPHY

1. Jeffrey M. Jones, *Record High in U.S. Say Big Government Greatest Threat* (Gallup.com, December 18, 2013).

2. Michael Hayden, Stanley McChrystal and James Stravidis, *One Small Change to Fix Our Broken Political System* (Time Magazine, June 15, 2015).

3. John Samples, *James Madison and the Future of Limited Government* (Cato Institute, June 14, 2002). 33.

4. Drew Desilver, *U.S. voter turnout trails most developed countries* (Pew Research Center, May 6, 2015).

5. Thomas Paine, *Common Sense, Rights of Man, and other essential writings of Thomas Paine* (Signet Classics, July 2003). 4-5.

6. Jeffrey M. Jones, *Confidence in U.S. Institutions Still Below Historical Norms* (Gallup.com, June 15, 2015).

7. Tiffany Kafer, *Constituents' right to speak causes disagreement* (Isanti-Chisago County Star, August 23, 2012).

8. Issie Lapowsky, *Political Ad Spending Online is about to Explode* (Wired.com, August 8, 2015). http://www.wired.com/2015/08/digital-politcal-ads-2016/

9. Art Swift, *Honesty and Ethics Rating of Clergy Slides to New Low* (Gallup.com, December 16, 2013). http://www.gallup.com/poll/166298/honesty-ethics-rating-clergy-slides-new-low.aspx

10. Elizabeth Sias, *Isanti County Board approves 1.5 percent increase in salaries* (Isanti County News, January 9, 2013).

11. John Samples, *James Madison and the Future of Limited Government* (Cato Institute, June 14, 2002). 135.

12. John Samples, *James Madison and the Future of Limited Government* (Cato Institute, June 14, 2002). 180.

13. Kyle Pomerleau, *Corporate Income Tax Rates around the World, 2015* (TaxFoundation.org, October 1, 2015).

14. John S. Kiernan, *2016's States with the Highest & Lowest Tax Rates* (WalletHub.com).

15. *Historical Expenditures: General Fund and All Funds* (mn.gov, March 14, 2016). http://mn.gov/mmb/images/feb16-historical.pdf

16. Shane Tritsch, *Why is Illinois So Corrupt?* (Politics & City Life, December 9, 2010).

17. Rachel Kytonen, *Isanti County Details 2016 Budget, Levy* (Isanti County News, December 9, 2015).

18. Phil Rogers and Patrick McCraney, *Entire Park District Board Placed Under Citizen's Arrest* (NBCChicago.com, published June 25, 2014). http://www.nbcchicago.com/investigations/Entire-Park-District-Board-Placed-Under-Citizens-Arrest-264660331.html

19. Contributor, *Minnesota's Lack of Transparency and Legislator Per Diem Pay* (AlphaNews.com, February 9, 2016).

20. L. Robert Kohls, *America's Thirteen Core Values* (The Washington International Center, April 1984).

21. John Samples, *James Madison and the Future of Limited Government* (Cato Institute, June 14, 2002). 27.

22. Becky Glander, *Isanti County sets 1.7 percent levy* (Isanti-Chisago County Star, September 15, 2009).

23. Tom Steward, *Landmark Ruling as Court Finds Victoria City Officials Committed 38 Open Meeting Law Violations* (Center of the American Experiment, April 1, 2016).

24. *Code of Ethics for Pharmacists* (Pharmacist.com, October 27, 1994). http://www.pharmacist.com/code-ethics

25. *BBB Standards for Trust* (bbb.org). https://www.bbb.org/council/about/vision-mission-and-values/bbb-standards-for-trust/

About the Author

ALAN DUFF SERVED TWENTY-THREE YEARS in military leadership, retiring as a Major in 2005. He then served six years as an elected official in local government. Duff founded Duff Companies, LLC in 2009 and currently serves as President of this company. His education includes a BS in political science, and a master's degree in urban and regional management.

Duff has extensive experience advocating for our nation's veterans at state and federal capitals. In 2013, he was awarded the Veteran Advocate for the Year award from the *Minneapolis St. Paul Business Journal*. He currently lives in Isanti, Minnesota.

Further information on Alan Duff can be found at MajorDuff.com

Made in the USA
San Bernardino, CA
23 August 2017